SHATTERED YET UNBROKEN

FINDING STRENGTH AND PURPOSE AFTER SUDDEN LOSS

MARCIA N. COLE

ISBN # 979-8-9925728-0-3

First printing, 2025.

Contents

INTRODUCTION...1

CHAPTER ONE: THE DAY OUR LIVES CHANGED FOREVER............4

CHAPTER TWO: HOW DID WE END UP HERE?.........................13

CHAPTER THREE: HOW DO I GET THROUGH THIS?...........21

CHAPTER FOUR: YOU CAN'T HAVE OUR MEMORIES.......................30

CHAPTER FIVE: MAKING THE PAIN LESS......................................40

CHAPTER SIX: MOVING THROUGH GRIEF WITH FAMILY.............50

CHAPTER SEVEN: ME, MYSELF, AND GRIEF.............................. 64

CHAPTER EIGHT: NEGATIVE OUTCOMES OF DOMESTIC
     VIOLENCE 77

CHAPTER NINE: FORGIVENESS 83

CHAPTER TEN: THE WORLD THAT ALWAYS FAILS 90

CHAPTER ELEVEN: THE ONE WHO NEVER FAILS...........................96

CHAPTER TWELVE: HONORING.. 106

CONCLUSION: A JOURNEY OF GRIEF AND HOPE 123

RESOURCES 128

Introduction

For everything there is a season, a time for every activity under heaven. A time to be born and a time to die. A time to plant and a time to harvest. A time to kill and a time to heal. A time to tear down and a time to build up. A time to cry and a time to laugh. A time to grieve and a time to dance. A time to scatter stones and a time to gather stones. A time to embrace and a time to turn away. A time to search and a time to quit searching. A time to keep and a time to throw away. A time to tear and a time to mend. A time to be quiet and a time to speak. A time to love and a time to hate. A time for war and a time for peace. What do people really get for all their hard work? I have seen the burden God has placed on us all. Yet God has made everything beautiful for its own time. He has planted eternity in the human heart, but even so, people cannot see the whole scope of God's work from beginning to end.

Ecclesiastes 3:1-11 NLT

The day we have to say goodbye is never easy or predictable. The moment someone we love transitions to heaven, the world shifts, and we're left grappling with the weight of their absence. They're no longer physically here to hold, laugh with, or talk to, and that is a gut-wrenching reality that we have to accept. It feels like a piece of our very soul has been taken, leaving a void that can never quite be filled. We are forced to face a new reality-a life on earth without that person by our side. Even though they are no longer physically with us, their voice, light, and purpose can continue to shine and inspire, refusing to fade away.

I believe that their legacy can still live on powerfully. It's my mission to be my brother's voice and to help others understand the power of being the voice for their loved ones-especially for those whose deaths could have been prevented. I want the world to see that our loved ones' lives, no matter how tragically cut short, still hold value and meaning. My prayer is that Dante's life, his spirit, and his purpose will continue to have an impact far beyond his years on this earth. Your loved one's voice does not have to be silent; you can be the vessel that keeps their life's purpose breathing, ensuring that their impact continues to resonate.

In this book, I will take you on my journey of navigating the grief of losing my brother, Dante. Let me tell you upfront-writing this book wasn't easy. Reliving the pain, the memories, and the reality of this loss over and over while writing this book has been a constant reminder that God is my source, my refuge, and my strength. I won't sugarcoat it: This is a heavy and emotional read. There are moments in these pages that will break your heart, because they've shattered mine. So, I'm going to say this from the start-have those tissues ready. Yes, ladies... and fellas, I'm talking to you, too. The weight of this story is undeniable, but it is a weight that needs to be carried, because the truth deserves to be told-not only for my brother, but for so many others like him. I couldn't sit back and let his story remain untold. I know there is freedom, healing, and hope in these pages-hope that someone else out there will see themselves, see their pain, and know they are not alone. I hope my story will shine a light in the darkest corners of grief, giving those who are mourning the courage to face their pain and find a way to live again. My sincere prayer is that my experiences provide solace, understanding, and guidance to those who are also navigating the turbulent waters of grief. I hope my story serves as a lifeline, a source of comfort, and a testimony to the healing power of God's love. Together, we will navigate the sorrow, honor those we've lost, and find a way to move forward without letting go of the love that will forever be a part of us..

You don't have to walk this road alone. With God, we will make it through, step by step, day by day. Let's do this together. Are you ready to take this journey with me?

CHAPTER ONE

The Day Our Lives Changed Forever

"I am leaving you with a gift—peace of mind and heart. And the peace I give is a gift the world cannot give. So don't be troubled or afraid."

John 14:27 (NLT)

The Weight of Loss

Another year has passed, and it still feels like yesterday. Some days I am still in disbelief. Sometimes I get this feeling that he will walk through the door, call my phone or send me a text. Family gatherings and celebrations are not the same. Life is not the same. I now must learn to live without him being present and cherish the moments we shared. One moment of rage can turn into a lifetime of pain. To most August 12, 2020 was a normal summer day but for my family, it was the worst day of our lives. It was the day my brother's life was violently stolen from him and those who deeply loved him. And to think this was right in the middle of a global pandemic, and when so many were already dealing with loss and grief from COVID.

"The doctors said they did all they could do but could not stop the bleeding!" Those were the words that echoed out of my mom's friend's mouth over the phone. Wait, this must be a dream, this can't be real. Somebody wake me up. They can't be talking about my brother. No, not my twenty-two-year-old brother. Not my heart, my everything, the very first man I ever loved. This could not be happening. This cannot be real. Dante, you must walk out of this hospital. These doctors must have the wrong person. Are they talking about Dante Eyasu? Am I dreaming? When am I going to wake up from this nightmare? He had so much life to live. He had just started a business, and things were looking amazing for the future. I was so proud of him. What is happening? God where are you? I knew God was going to turn this around for his good. I knew God was only giving him a mighty testimony. That this was going to be the thing that finally helped him walk away from this toxic relationship. I just knew God had other plans, and at this time, I just didn't know how this was going to work for my good. Why is it that what the enemy meant for evil-my brother's girlfriend stabbing and killing him-would lead to God working out for good?

The Call That Changed Everything

It was on August 12, 2020 at 8:14pm, time stood still. I felt numb. Nothing could compare to the hurt and pain that stabbed me right in the middle of my soul. It was like an out of body experience. I could not breathe. I could not fully comprehend what I was hearing. I had faith, I knew God was going to see him through. I was so confident this was just a part of his testimony, and he would be okay. I never could have imagined this happening. Not to us, not now. I have experienced the effects of death before but not like this.

It was like any other day. I was at home working when I received a call from my sister asking me to call my brother. He and his girlfriend were at my mom's house arguing again, all while my dad and my sister's boyfriend were in the house. My sister left the house not too long before and had just missed my brother. Her boyfriend had called to tell her what was going on. This wasn't new, they argued often. We would normally be the ones to intervene and try to calm the situation down. My sister and I, along with several other family members and his friends, tried so hard to convince Dante to leave this relationship. IT

WAS VERY TOXIC. He would always say, "Yall don't understand; y'all don't see her like I do; she's not a bad person. You just have to get to know her better". Believe me, I did understand. I had several conversations with her. I knew something was off, but I couldn't put my hands on it. She did seem like a really nice girl who stayed to herself, at least while around me.

But during several conversations in person and via text something just felt off. And I heard several stories about her from my brother's friends and believe me she was not quiet or no one's angel. I mean we all have a side to us that's not always revealed to the public, but my sister and I knew something was off. Oh, and let me mention-we both work in the mental health field. Dante felt he could change her, and he was all she had, which was a lie she made him believe.

Getting a call informing me that my brother and his girlfriend were arguing was nothing out of the ordinary. That day, I decided to allow them to figure it out as I couldn't continue to run to the rescue. They would typically fight, break up and then get back together. It was like a cycle of dysfunction. But who would have known that this day would be different. This wouldn't be just an argument. A few minutes after the first call, I received another call from my sister telling me that my brother had been stabbed by his girlfriend. She was very hysterical. I thought she said he got stabbed in the back. I immediately got up to leave my house to head toward my parents' house, which is where the incident took place. I told my kids I had an emergency and had to leave the house. Surprisingly I was very calm, as I had this confidence that he would be okay. Once I got in the car, I immediately contacted all the prayer warriors I knew and asked them to start calling out his name in prayer for God to bring my brother through. While driving to my parent's house, I was making calls and praying to God to save him and see him through. My sister and I were on the phone calling the house trying to figure out what was happening. Dante isn't answering his phone. Our dad isn't answering the phone. It took several times before we got our dad to finally answer. We just wanted to know what was happening. Was Dante okay? Was he talking? Was he bleeding? Did anyone call 9-1-1? Our dad was no help as he was in shock. He was not giving us any real answers. By the time we talked to him, the ambulance and police were there.

We couldn't understand why they were just at the house and not on the way to the hospital. Why were they not moving? They finally left after what seemed like forever. We still didn't know how our brother was. After we got the information and which hospital they were heading to, we drove straight there. It didn't take us long to get there, as it was close to my parents' house. My drive from my house to the hospital was about 45 minutes and my sister was close to an hour away. Another call I had to make, which I was dreading, was to my mom- who was at work at the time everything took place. I had to be careful with my words so I wouldn't send her into a panic. Luckily for me, she was already off the clock headed home. She was surprisingly very calm when I told her to meet me at the hospital because Dante was stabbed by his girlfriend.

Making Peace with Pain

Once I parked at the hospital, I headed straight to the ER. The receptionist could not provide me with any updates, so I waited and went back to ask questions every few minutes. When I finally got an update, he was in imaging, and eventually would undergo surgery. My mom, sister, and childhood friends arrived at the hospital shortly after. Due to COVID restrictions, only one person would wait in the operating room (OR) waiting room for the surgeons to provide updates. My mom went inside while we all stayed outside. During this time, we reflected on the memories of my brother growing up and discussed what led us to this point of waiting outside of a hospital. At times I would walk away from the group to talk to God. I prayed continuously. I listened to worship music. I knew deep in my heart that God was going to see him through this situation. I knew he was going to be okay. I continued to repeat, "Lord, bring him home. He shall live and not die". During my prayer and repeating that phrase, I was stopped in my thoughts with the following thought, "Marcia you are asking God to bring him home but if He comes to heaven he does go home to be with God. You're saying he shall live and not die, if he comes to heaven he is living." I just knew in my soul that the Lord would see him through to the other side of this; that he would see him in a mighty way and see his story help others in similar situations. I felt that this was just a part of his story, and that God was going to give him a mighty testimony. We waited for what felt like eternity. No updates. My mom continued to watch the OR board in the waiting room.

We continued to call the OR asking for an update. Family and close friends continued to show up to the hospital for support. This is how good God is. Before, I said only my mom was allowed to wait in the waiting room due to COVID restrictions. Somehow her close girlfriend was able to get into the hospital and be by her side during the wait and the impending devastating news. I was on the phone with my mom's friend when the doctors were walking out with an update. I could barely hear what they were saying. I had to ask my mom's friend to repeat it. I will never forget the heart-wrenching words that came out of her mouth next, "He did not make it. They said they tried to do as much as they could, but he lost too much blood, and it was hard to reach the cut artery to stop the bleeding." Nothing could prepare me for the words that echoed from the surgeon's mouth. I just needed someone to pinch me, to wake me up from this nightmare. My brother, not my brother...Dante, come back please. Dante this can't be real. God why? Why Dante why? I was speechless. I was numb. I was in shock.

I walked to an empty area in the parking lot, fell to my knees and just cried and screamed out loud. All I could hear around me was my family and friends crying, screaming and in pure shock. When I was finally able to pick myself up off the ground, I knew I needed to find my mom and dad. My sister and I were outside with each other surrounded by family and friends. My mom was still inside and eventually made it outside with us. I know it was only the Lord that was holding her up. For her to be able to walk out of that hospital, it was only God. My brother was her baby and only son.

Unfortunately, our dad was at the police station talking to the detectives helping them with their investigation. Do you know the detectives find out ASAP when someone passes even before the family? So, the detective who was with our dad knew my brother had passed hours before us and they were still trying to keep him. I was furious when I came to this realization. When we called him to tell him to come to the hospital, the detectives kept trying to keep him so I felt bad but I had to tell him over the phone so he could understand why we needed him at the hospital. This was not supposed to happen, those words were not supposed to come out of my mouth. That call should have been 'Dante made it out of surgery'. Even as I'm writing these words, I can still feel the pain of that day as if I'm walking in it right now.

Lord, why is this my new truth?

Our Special Bond

My brother was about thirteen years younger than me. We spent a lot of time together; it was like he was attached to my hip. Wherever I went he would follow. My brother moved in with my family and I during his high school years to attend school in my area - which would provide a better education. During that time, our bond became stronger. He was more like a brother to my kids than their uncle. He was always at my house on the weekends and during school breaks. I know for sure if we lived closer to my parent's house, he would have been there every day.

I never would have imagined we would be here, or that I would experience what I experienced on August 12, 2020. To now have to speak about my brother in the past tense and saying he was MURDERED was not an easy reality to accept. Somewhere in between the various emotions I felt that day, I felt a little peace. I have yet to gather words to explain it. I thanked God for his life, I told God I forgive my brother's girlfriend for taking my heart, my everything, my brother away from his family. I then proceeded to ask God how are we going to turn this around for good? How are you going to use me to make sure my brother's death is not in vain? I needed to know HOW. How was this going to turn around for good? Just as Dante would always say, God whispered to me, "I got you." See, in life we face many trials and tribulations that knock us down and can make us want to give up. We feel alone and numb. As much as it hurts, as much as it doesn't make sense, God still has a plan. God, and only God, can turn anything around for us.

Finding Purpose in Pain

In the days, hours, and minutes after my brother's transition, I felt more peace and understanding from God like never before. Yes, my brother was only 22 and still had so much more life to live, but he accomplished more in his 22 years than most people will in their 50, 60, and even 80 years here on earth. His character spoke for itself, he had a beautiful soul and an infectious smile. He was the true definition of selfless as he made any stranger feel loved.

I didn't know that God was preparing me for this moment in more ways than one. The day before my brother was murdered, I started an Instagram Live Series on forgiveness. And the next day, I would be tested on everything I was teaching others to do. As much as it hurts, because I want my brother back here on earth, I chose to forgive his girlfriend. Nothing has changed from the night the surgeons said, "we tried everything." Even at that moment, I whispered, "I forgive you". I refuse to harbor hate and unforgiveness in my heart as all it does is keep me from the promises of God. I chose to go after the real enemy, I chose to trust God and lean on His promises of victory. I'm preparing myself for the fight with God as my commander. The enemy comes to steal, kill and destroy by using others and I refuse to give him the glory or give him the victory. It's time to take back territory that has always belonged to us. It's time to put the enemy right where he belongs-beneath us. The enemy will not take anyone or anything else from me. Enough is enough.

Unbroken Key Takeaways

- Grief is unpredictable and doesn't follow a set timeline. Some days it feels like yesterday, and other days it feels like an eternity.

- Toxic relationships can be blinding—love sometimes makes it hard to see the truth, but ignoring red flags can lead to devastating consequences.

- The weight of loss is heavy, but we are not meant to carry it alone. God is present, even when we don't understand His plans.

- In moments of crisis, faith is tested. It's easy to believe when everything is going well, but true faith is believing even when it feels like everything is falling apart.

- The power of prayer is real, but God's answers may not always align with our expectations. Even in the deepest pain, His presence remains.

Unbroken Reflection Questions

1. Have you ever believed that God would turn a situation around, only for it to end differently than expected? How did that impact your faith?

2. What does "making peace with pain" look like for you? Are you allowing yourself to heal, or are you carrying the weight alone?

3. How can you lean into God's presence even when life feels unbearable?

CHAPTER TWO

How Did We End Up Here?

"Guard your heart above all else, for it determines the course of your life."

Proverbs 4:23 (NLT)

The Warning Sign

Time after time, I found myself tirelessly attempting to convince Dante that he needed to break free from the suffocating grip of this toxic relationship. It was evident to me that the bond they shared was far from healthy, and there had to be better ways for them to communicate and connect. Yet, no matter how much I pleaded with him, he remained steadfast in his defense of her, proclaiming, "You guys just don't understand. She's actually a good person deep down, and she can be really nice." It was a frustrating loop, leaving me feeling helpless and desperate to make him see the reality of the situation. I even had several conversations with her, telling her to just leave him alone, block him and stop reaching out. I told her that their relationship was not healthy at all.

I tried my best to be careful with my words, ensuring he knew I wasn't out to demonize her. I'd tell him, "I'm not trying to say she's a bad person, but right now, you need to focus on yourself and find your own happiness before you can even think about trying to fix this relationship". The depth of her emotional manipulation knew no bounds. She managed to make him believe that he was her sole lifeline, her only source of love in this world. The mere thought of him leaving her would drive her to threaten suicide, leaving him feeling trapped and responsible for her well-being. Countless times, he mustered the courage to walk away, only to receive a call filled with desperate cries, saying things like, "No one loves you. You're the only one that cares about me. I'm going to hurt myself." He felt obligated to stay, as if he were the only one capable of saving her from herself, and no one else could possibly understand her like he did.

Family Intervention Attempts

As his family and friends, we saw the toll this relationship took on him. We knew the incredible person he was, the love and care he had to offer, and we saw him being drained emotionally and mentally. We continuously urged him that she wasn't the right fit for him, that he deserved someone who would cherish and respect him. However, the more we tried to pry them apart, the more entangled they became.

Over the years, we learned of the various ways she played a part in the unfortunate events that unfolded in his life. Even before he transitioned, she left a trail of destruction, weaving herself into a web of malevolence in his life. One incident revealed she played a role in a past altercation, which left him with haunting scars, both physical and emotional. When we told him about it, he was in denial. He couldn't bring himself to believe it was true. His incident almost killed him and caused him great physical and emotional harm. Her actions were malicious, deceitful, and manipulative, as she betrayed his trust time and time again.

Despite countless interventions, we struggled to make him realize that this relationship was nothing short of toxic. We-his family, his confidantes, his support system-had endless conversations with him, urging him to break free from this harmful connection. My sister, my mom, my aunt, and I all tried to make him see the light, but it was as if he was spellbound, unable to see the damage she was inflicting upon him. My husband and I had countless conversations with Dante, trying to help him see what we saw. He would listen, and it seemed like he understood, but somehow, he always ended up back with her. I even had my husband's friend, who had been in a similar relationship and was able to get out of it, talk to Dante. He listened to him too, but again, nothing changed. The hardest part was when her own sister told Dante to leave her, that she wasn't good for him. And yet, he stayed. It was like no matter how much we tried to reach him, something kept pulling him back.

I found myself rushing to her house on numerous occasions, picking him up after yet another heated argument. We'd talk, and he'd swear he would cut ties with her, delete her number, and ignore her calls. Yet, somehow, she'd manage to creep back into his life, and he'd find himself entangled in her web once more. I'll never forget a conversation I had with her that left me speechless and filled with a deep sense of urgency. She told me that sometimes she would blackout, and when that happened, anything could happen—but that wasn't the part that truly scared me. It was the way she was laughing and smirking as she said it, almost as if she found it amusing. In that moment, I knew something was deeply wrong, not just with the situation, but with her. I immediately called my sister and told her, "We need to get Dante away from her. Something is seriously off here." I couldn't shake the feeling that this was more than just a warning; it was a red flag we couldn't ignore.

Feeling increasingly powerless, I turned to prayer, hoping that maybe through divine intervention, something would change. I sought to empower him to focus on his own happiness, his dreams, and the things that brought him joy. My hope was that he'd begin to recognize his worth and understand that he deserved a healthy, loving relationship, free from manipulation and fear. That whatever was broken in him would be made whole and he would understand what it truly means to love yourself.

The Role of Mental Health

I believe if we love ourselves then we understand how to love others. We can't love others if we don't first love God and ourselves. I'm a true believer that everyone needs therapy as we all have some childhood trauma we did to heal from. Of course, JESUS AND THERAPY. Therapy not only helps us on a healing journey, but it can also provide us with healthy tools for communication, navigating relationships and conflicts. Unfortunately, in our society therapy is frowned upon and not fully understood, especially amongst black men. Therapy is not their first or second option. Some of our black men are raised to just deal with their emotions and suck it up. Some of our black men are not taught how to effectively regulate their emotions and even raised to think their feelings don't matter. So, they tend to hide, reject and suppress their feelings, which eventually builds up inside and turns into anger and causing them to be constantly misunderstood. The other problem is we as women feel we can fix and change them which isn't the truth.

As women, we sometimes enable the negative behaviors and coping patterns. Their built-up anger and frustration is what often leads them to being verbally and physically abusive. Let me just pause and say this to the women-We need to learn how to just be silent and listen to our men. The said and the unsaid things. We need to create a safe place for them to be vulnerable and not judge them for how they feel. We have to hold them accountable and give them grace, but do not continue to encourage the bad behaviors. Sometimes walking away and leaving is the best thing you can do in a toxic environment. We do not always have to have the last word and prove we are right. Most times the best proof is in our actions not our words.

Societal Perspectives

It's disheartening that society often lays the sole blame on the man in toxic relationships, failing to acknowledge the emotional manipulation and abuse that women are capable of inflicting. Emotional manipulation can be just as damaging as physical violence, as it tears at the very core of a person's self-worth. Her tactics were insidious, degrading him and messing with his mind, while simultaneously professing love and affection. To just sit and hear the crazy, and sometimes terrifying, things she did from my brothers' friends and even him left me in shock. It almost felt like I was watching a Lifetime movie unfold right before me. It wasn't just her actions, but also how he continued to allow himself to be in this type of relationship. This wasn't healthy at all. This wasn't love. But this was reality- not just for my brother and her, but for many others in the world. From putting sugar in his gas tank to showing up at his friend's house with threats of violence, she reveled in asserting her control over him. Signs of her instability were evident, and we tried to tell him that he wasn't the person equipped to heal her. He needed help seeing that something within him was broken and needed to be healed and rebuilt. When there are two unhealed people in a relationship, they typically are not truly in love but bonded by similar trauma and hurt. This only leads to a continuously dysfunctional and toxic cycle. Things will seem good, then they are bad, then good again, then bad again; and you seem to never have a sense of peace no matter what you try to do. This requires one to first fix what's broken inside of them, not "fix" the other person. The hardest thing for some people to realize is the only person they could ever change and/or fix is themselves.

The Fatal Turning Point

The day he was taken away from us changed everything, yet it was calm. As I later heard, from our dad and my sister's boyfriend, my brother was surprisingly composed, telling his girlfriend that he was done and taking her home, and his girlfriend was continuously arguing and provoking him. He was trying to relax and spend time at our parents' house since it was his day off. He did not have any intention to argue or provoke her, just a desire to move on. We believe he had finally reached a point where he was done with this toxic cycle. We believe she thought about it and planned to hurt my brother. The knife she used to stab him came from my parent's kitchen, but they weren't in the kitchen when it happened. At some point she went into the kitchen, got the knife and hid it on her. We strongly believe it was premeditated; she had time to think about what she would do. She wasn't being threatened nor kept against her will. If she felt she was in danger, she could have called the cops or run down the street to the police station. Let's not forget she was in the house with two other people; she was not alone with my brother. He was the one in danger and did not even know it. She was plotting on him right before his eyes and in his family's home. Tragically, some individuals can't bear the thought of being rejected, leading to devastating outcomes. Let's be honest, rejection is not easy for anyone. It does not feel good and can be a very hard pill to swallow. When you have other unresolved trauma and hurt, being rejected may cause you to snap. We hear about it all the time, sadly because of the devastating outcomes. Hopefully, we will have more families and survivors raising their voices, and those who need help will get help sooner to avoid this pain. People first have to come to the understanding that they only have control over themselves.

We are not responsible for anyone's healing but our own.

Dante's girlfriend was not a stranger, and this was not a random act. She was someone he loved and cared about. She would come to my house and family gatherings. She lived in the same neighborhood as my mother-in-love, literally right in the same complex. You could see her house from my mother-in-love's house. Her sisters went to the same school as my kids.

In hindsight, I often wonder if there was more that I could have done, if different words or actions could have altered the course of events. I wrestle with a mix of emotions—sadness, regret, and guilt-wishing I could have somehow rescued him from the darkness that consumed him. I tried my best with the resources and abilities available to me, but ultimately, they were two adults responsible for their choices. Despite the heartbreak, I find solace in knowing that I can use this experience to raise awareness about domestic violence, especially when it pertains to men. It is vital that we support our loved ones who may be trapped in such situations, help them heal from past traumas, and foster healthy relationships.

Through sharing this deeply personal story, I hope to inspire others to be empathetic, understanding, and proactive when confronting toxic relationships. By advocating for change, we can create a society where love is pure, and relationships are built on mutual respect, trust, and genuine care for one another. Where people are able to quickly identify toxic patterns in themselves and others in order to get the support and help they greatly need.

Unbroken Key Takeaways

- True love does not manipulate, control, or threaten. When a relationship causes more harm than good, it is not love but an unhealthy attachment.

- No matter how much you want to help someone, they must make the choice to walk away from toxicity and toward healing.

- Repeated emotional manipulation, threats, and toxic behaviors are clear indicators of danger. Red flags should never be rationalized or overlooked.

- Society often disregards or downplays the abuse men endure, but emotional and psychological abuse can be just as damaging as physical abuse.

- Two broken people cannot "fix" each other. True healing requires self-awareness, personal accountability, and often professional help.

- Staying in a toxic relationship out of obligation or fear can have fatal consequences. Knowing when to walk away is a sign of strength, not weakness.

Unbroken Reflection Questions

1. What are some red flags you've ignored in past relationships or friendships? What did you learn from those experiences?

2. Have you ever found yourself trying to "fix" or "save" someone in a relationship? What was the outcome?

3. What does Proverbs 4:23 ("Guard your heart above all else, for it determines the course of your life.") mean to you in the context of relationships?

CHAPTER THREE

How Do I Get Through This?

"Jesus looked at them and said, "With man this is impossible, but with God all things are possible."

Matthew 19:26 NIV

Finding God In Grief

Listen, if it wasn't for God on my side, I do not know where I would be. I've never felt a loss like this before. It hurt. It hurt really bad, no one could comfort me or speak words that would make me feel better. To be honest, at times, I didn't think I would get through this. The only thing that comforted me was the fact that God blessed me with 22 years of good memories with my brother. I found so many moments of peace by just being grateful for the time we had together. I find comfort in knowing that God was going to use my brother's story to save others. I kept repeating "one life for a million…one life for a million". I found comfort in knowing that prior to my brother's transition, he was able to accomplish so much at such a young age. I could not process this as I previously processed other challenges or tough seasons in my life. God told me to sit still, not to rush my healing, but to sit in it and allow myself to feel every emotion, and not to run and hide from this. I was so used to just moving and not processing. I was used to being strong. I was used to having all the answers, but this time it was different. I needed more. I couldn't do this alone. I needed God and God is all I needed. Nothing could ease my pain. Nothing else could wipe away my tears.

Only God could comfort me and help me make it to the other side of this pain. I know there was something on the other side, but I didn't fully understand how I was going to make it. I just needed to be in His presence and seated at His feet. Like in the story of Lazarus, in the bible, I had to be like Mary and not Martha. I was so accustomed to being like Martha. But I had to stay at the feet of Jesus, trusting fully in Him and not my own understanding. His presence was the only thing that could get me through this trying time in my life. Healing and understanding were not going to come from others or the busyness of life, but just by being at His feet.

Understanding The Grief Journey

When I think about grief the first word that comes to mind is rollercoaster. Grief is an ever-surprising emotional rollercoaster. You never know when it's going to make you cry, bring on instant sadness, anger, or even a state of confusion. The hardest part of this tragedy that we were walking through was the reality of Dante being murdered at such a young tender age and brutally ripped away from us at the hands of someone who was supposed to love him. Our family was already grieving the passing of other family members. My brother's life wasn't snatched away by a stranger, nor was this an accident; and now two families have changed forever.

There were times I would feel shame and guilt. Times I would question my position in my brother's life. I would ask myself questions like, "did my brother know I loved him? Did he feel supported? Did he feel appreciated?" Maybe I was too hard at times. Maybe I should have done more. You know, all of the should of, could of, would of scenarios; all of the lies and overwhelming thoughts the enemy tries to fill your head with. One day I said enough is enough and told the enemy to get ye behind me. I told him out loud, I did the best I could with what I knew with my brother. I loved him immensely. What happened to him is not my fault but your fault. You are the one who comes to steal, kill & destroy, but you can't take my joy. You can't take away the memories. I have what most will never have. I had 22, almost 23 years with my brother filled with some of the most memorable moments. I will not allow you to take this away from me, you will not get the glory. I will continue to thank God every day of my life.

Losing my brother to murder has been one of the hardest things I've ever had to face, and the journey through it has been a mix of pain, growth, and finding ways to navigate a life that's forever changed. In all of this, I hold on to the truth that I believe in Jesus, therapy, and community. Even now, sometimes I find myself floating through life-moving, but not really present. It's like I'm physically here, but my mind and heart are still grappling with the reality that my brother is gone. I often catch myself thinking, "I can't believe this happened to Dante. He should still be here." And then, I close my eyes, and I can see him, feel him-his smile, oh, that smile.

The Three Pillars of Healing

It's a strange thing, grief. Sometimes it feels like you're stuck in a

fog, unable to see anything clearly, yet somehow you keep going. But for me, leaning on faith, therapy, and a strong community made all the difference. These have been the anchors that have kept me from being swallowed whole by the pain of my brother's loss. Therapy, in particular, played a major role in my healing. I didn't jump into therapy right away—I needed to sit in my pain for a while, to really process everything. My first therapy session was at the end of November, nearly four months after Dante passed. This wasn't my first time going to therapy, but it felt different this time. I knew it was the best next step in my healing journey. I'm incredibly thankful to God for guiding me to the woman He sent my way.

Let me tell you, finding a therapist during the end of 2020 was no easy task. So many people were turning to therapy, trying to heal from the grief and the uncertainty the year brought, due to the COVID-19 pandemic. A lot of therapists had long waiting lists, but God made a way for me to connect with someone who was a perfect fit. When I started searching, I had a certain criterion. I wanted a Christian woman who specialized in grief, and God gave me exactly that. My therapist not only met my requirements, but she exceeded them. From the moment we started, she set the tone. Before even beginning our sessions, she wanted to meet with me to make sure we were a good match. That was a first for me, and it gave me such peace. From there, we started working, and I've been grateful ever since.

She's helped me in more ways than I can express. She's brought me back to the word of God and prayer-which I didn't realize I desperately needed. There were moments when I didn't have the strength to pray on my own, and she would pray for me in our sessions. It felt like a lifeline. She reminded me of who God is and how He holds me, even in this pain. She didn't just let me stay stuck in my grief-she challenged my emotions with truth. She also gave me biblical guidance and understanding that helped me navigate this complicated journey. And most importantly, she always led me back to Jesus. I always leave therapy feeling lighter, with a sense of relief, ready to face whatever lies ahead.

Now, let me be real, therapy hasn't always been easy. Who likes hearing hard truths, right? But even though those truths stung, they were exactly what I needed to hear. Therapy opened my eyes to new perspectives, showing me the truth even when it was uncomfortable. It helped me process, heal, and move forward. But I won't sugarcoat it; therapy requires work. It doesn't work unless you put in the effort. You have to be honest with yourself, willing to face the hard truths, and let go of the things holding you back. You have to forgive, even when it feels impossible. Therapy isn't a quick fix; it's a journey. And finding the right therapist is key. Not every therapist is the right fit, and that's okay. You just have to find your person.

One of the most important things my therapist taught me early on was: *You are not responsible for other people's grief.* That one hit me hard. We often think we have to carry the weight of everyone else's emotions, but we can't. Another lesson was to *give myself grace.* Grief doesn't look the same for everyone, and it's okay to feel however you feel. And lastly, she taught me to *be honest with myself about how I was feeling, even when it didn't make sense or when it was too painful to admit.*

Community was also a huge part of my healing process. When you're grieving, it can feel so isolating, but being surrounded by people who understand, who love you, and who don't shy away from your pain makes all the difference. Family and friends became my lifeline. They wrapped their arms around us, and even when we didn't ask for help, they showed up. They came to our house, sat with us, cooked for us, and simply were just there for us. They didn't just disappear after the funeral-they continued to check in on us, and they still do. It's that kind of love that helps you keep going, even when you feel like you can't. In the early days after Dante's death, people came together in ways I'll never forget. Family, friends, and even people who didn't live close by-some drove over an hour just to sit with us, bringing food, offering prayers, and simply being there. They helped us plan the funeral and contributed toward the expenses. The outpouring of love from our community was overwhelming in the best possible way.

Towards the end of 2020, I also joined an online grief group called Journey to Restoration. We met weekly on Zoom, and the sessions were led by a Christian therapist who understood grief on a personal level. These sessions were so healing—being able to talk to others who had experienced a loss like mine gave me a sense of comfort I hadn't found elsewhere. We would lean into the word of God and share our struggles, and it was always a space where I could express myself freely without fear of judgment. It wasn't easy, and it still isn't. But the combination of Jesus, therapy, and community has been my anchor. They've carried me through some of my darkest days, reminding me that healing is possible, even in the deepest pain. I don't have all the answers, and I'm still healing, but I know that I don't have to walk this journey alone.

Navigating Daily Life

Some will tell you that time heals all wounds, and for me, I would agree to an extent. Yes, some things do get easier with time, but it's not about time passing on its own-it's about what you choose to focus on during that time. The pain may not go away completely, but you begin to learn how to live with it, how to carry it without it completely defining who you are. And yes, you do get better at preparing for the tough days-the anniversary of their death, their birthday, holidays, etc. But let's be real, even when you think you're prepared, some days still hit you harder than you expect. There are still times when I break down, when the grief is so heavy I can't breathe, when I ask God, "Why? Why him? Why us?" In those moments, I don't try to fight it. I just let myself be. I rest, I sit in silence, and sometimes, I let the tears flow because I've learned that crying isn't a sign of weakness-it's a part of healing. I allow myself to feel all the emotions without shame, to not rush through them. And when the grief feels too overwhelming, I lean into worship. I'll play some worship music and let the words lift me, even if I can't sing them myself. I've found that in worship, I find comfort even when I don't have the words to pray. Sometimes, a good movie or binge-watching a TV series helps too; just something to take my mind off the hurt for a while, even if it's just temporary. But what really helps, what truly brings me some relief, is being around people who know how to make me laugh. The people who remind me that it's okay to smile again, to find joy even in the midst of sadness.

Grief doesn't follow a linear path; it's not a neat and tidy process. Some days are better than others, and some days will knock you off your feet. But it's in those tough moments that I've learned to give myself permission to just be-to not always have to be strong or have it all together. And I've learned that it's okay to take my time, to heal at my own pace.

You may be in a place where you feel like you can't get past or get through this. I am here to tell you there is something on the other side of despair and sorrow. I'm not pushing you to rush or "forget". I'm telling you that you have something to look forward to. The pain never ends, you just learn to push through it. You must allow yourself to feel. You must allow yourself to process. I mean feel every emotion and not run from it. Try not to focus on other people's journeys, what they are saying, or even how they are processing. Focus on you, your journey and what you are feeling. It is easy for others to tell you how to feel or even how long you should grieve. Only you and that person who transitioned really know and understand the relationship you had.

Everyone grieves but everyone does not grieve the same; and as Christians, our way of grieving may look or feel different for another. You must figure out what works for you during your time in need. You need to develop positive coping skills, understanding there are some things that can help you heal but there are some things that will only cause deeper pain. You can heal. It is possible to feel joy again. It is possible to love again. You are still here on earth and there is more for you to accomplish. Your loved ones may be unavailable physically, but their spirit continues to live on through us who are left here on earth. You can help another person, to comfort another person, and maybe save another person. There is always a purpose for everything that happens in our life. You may not understand or can process it at this moment, but there is a purpose in physical death.

God was my first step to processing and moving through my grief.

Your first step may be something different, whatever step you take first, just take a step towards healing and moving through your grief. Every day is going to be different, sometimes it may be hour by hour. Just remember to continue to move forward. It doesn't have to be fast, just move. The more you continue to move forward, you will start to find peace little by little. What can you do today to move forward?

Unbroken Key Takeaways

- No words or actions from others could truly comfort the pain of loss, but God's presence brings peace.

- Grief comes with unexpected waves of emotions, and healing is not a straight path.

- Instead of rushing through grief, sitting in the emotions and trusting God's process leads to true healing.

- Leaning on God, seeking professional help, and having a strong support system are essential in navigating grief.

- Healing is a process that requires honesty, effort, and a willingness to face hard truths.

- It's okay to prioritize personal healing without carrying the emotional weight of others.

- Surrounding oneself with supportive people helps in the journey toward healing.

Unbroken Reflection Questions

1. In times of deep pain, where do you usually turn for comfort? How can you intentionally seek God's presence in those moments?

2. Have you ever felt guilty or questioned your actions after losing someone? How can you shift your perspective to focus on love and gratitude rather than regret?

3. What emotions have you avoided processing in your grief journey? What would it look like to allow yourself to fully feel them?

4. How do you view therapy? If you've never tried it, what are your hesitations, and how might it benefit your healing process?

5. In what ways has community played a role in your healing? How can you open yourself up to receiving or offering support?

6. What truth from Scripture can you hold onto when grief feels overwhelming?

7. How can you extend grace to yourself in your healing process, allowing room for both pain and progress?

CHAPTER FOUR

You Can't Have Our Memories

"But then I recall all you have done, O Lord; I remember your wonderful deeds of long ago."

Psalm 77:11 (NLT)

Early Memories

Memories, memory memories. I often just sit back, close my eyes and remember the laughs, the vacations, the family dinners, and the family outings we had. I am the first born with a younger sister, so when I found out I was having a baby brother, I was elated! I was headed into my freshman year of high school when he was born. Naturally, with the 13-year age gap, I knew having a younger sibling came with a large load, a list of responsibilities and the opportunity to be the "second Mom". That boy was attached to my hip and every time I left the house he would want to go. All of my friends knew him, and how he was a very active young boy. I remember when the movie *Friday* came out and easily became his favorite movie. This was back in the VHS days-you know before DVDs. His favorite part of the movie was when the husband ran out of the house chasing the other guy and one of them yelled "you got dang devil." He laughed every single time. I mean that rolling on the floor, laughing until you're crying kind of laugh. He just got such a kick out of that scene. Every chance he got he would try to watch the movie. Because it was so inappropriate for his age, we had to hide it from him, but somehow, he would always find it and I would always get in trouble because he found it. He was an adventurous kid, very active and all boy. He loved climbing, running and jumping off of things. You could not take your eyes off of him.

Growing Together

When I got older and moved out of the house, Dante came over almost every weekend. I can remember many snow days we had, and it was somehow only Dante, my kids and I at my house. My husband would have to stay at work because he was an essential worker. My brother, my children and I would have so much fun getting booted up to walk to a nearby store in a snowstorm. He was always so helpful when it came to cleaning off the cars and clearing the walking area. These are moments I adulate.

The fun continued when he started high school and officially moved in with us to attend the school in our county. During the week, it would usually be just me, my brother, and the kids, because of my husband's work schedule. We would have so much fun just being in the house or going out for family dinners. He always wanted to go to Bob Evans, which he loved. Every now and then they would have a 4-course meal option that he would always order.

Family Bonds

As he got older, he took on that big brother responsibility with my kids. If the kids needed something, he would be right there for them. I remember my son would call Dante to take him to 7-Eleven to get gift cards for his PlayStation. My husband and I would tell him, "No", but he would call Dante too and Dante would be right there to take him. He would come and say, "Did Charles tell you that he wanted to go to 7-Eleven to get a gift card?" I would say,' Yes, but we told him No!" That was Dante always coming to be there for the kids. Another time,

I had sent a text to Dante and my husband's brother to ask them to help my son as he was struggling with friendships at school and his self-esteem. Dante came to my house that evening to talk and spend time with him. He made sure to always be there for the kids, and anyone who was in need. He was very good at relating and encouraging others.

Let's get into family vacations! We come from a big family, and we have many traditions, like family reunions and annual family vacations. There are so many memories, and because we were so close, he was like my son and a brother to my kids. Every vacation I went on as an adult, my brother and my sister would be with us-every trip.

Dante had such a love for music. He didn't just listen to one genre of music but many different genres. He shared this love for music with my sister and daughter. He and my daughter would often just go for drives and listen to music. Dante loved riding; he didn't need to have a planned destination. It was so funny because he knew exactly what type of music to play for me while we were driving somewhere. He knew I loved gospel, neo-soul and R& B. He would play songs that came out years before he was even born and be jamming to it. I would ask him, "What do you know about this? How do you know this song?" He would just laugh and smile. If you're looking for a good movie or a good show to watch, Dante was the person to get some advice from. He would always say "Sis you got to watch this", and then he'll keep asking "Did you watch that?" Whenever I had downtime to watch TV, I would call to ask for a good recommendation because he recommended some really great shows.

Countless laughs, visits to amusement parks, park visits, movies watched, heated conversations and moments of love shared-we have so many great memories to cherish and hold on to forever. Even our little heated conversations when we're having a brother-sister moment, and I tried to get him on the right path or explain something to him were special. My sister and I still laugh about those moments.

Special Moments

There were countless times where my sister and I would be on a three-way call with our brother, and you could hear him say "Y'all just don't understand." We often responded with, "Yeah, I don't get it. Yeah, I just don't understand", and he would get so mad at us. We knew he would call us back at least one hour later and say, "You guys are right". And he would apologize for getting upset and not trying to hear our views. I would often remind him, we are not trying to be right, but we were just trying to help guide him in the right direction and open his eyes to the things he didn't see. Even now, there are times when my sister and I sit back and just reflect on some of our previous conversations with him. We realized even at his young age, he was full of such wisdom and knowledge. He made really great observations of things and people; he just didn't listen to his own words. Let's be honest, most of us don't. I am so grateful for being able to have experienced him in my life and that he was a part of our lives.

We often called him "our little Big brother" because he thought he knew more than us. Dante was always there for us, for whatever we needed. He went above and beyond a lot and we didn't really have to ask him for stuff because he would already just know and get it done. He was very good with his hands and fixing things-from things around the house to technology. He loved to help and found great joy in helping others.

Since he was the youngest and my only brother, he was spoiled by all of us. Whatever he needed we would provide. We would try to set limits and teach him how to be responsible, but we often would give in. For example, if he was not responsible with his spending, we would tell him we weren't going to Cash App or give him more money. It wasn't that he was carelessly spending money on clothes, shoes or what not; but he was mostly helping everyone else, and of course he loved to eat. He constantly tried to prove to us that he was being financially responsible and making good decisions. He would show me his transactions via his bank account to prove how he was spending his money. We wanted him to succeed at everything he did. As much as we constantly wanted to say "No", it was hard. I mean, he was my only little brother. I felt a strong need to always watch after him and be there for him.

His Generous Spirit

He would always talk about how one day he was going to take care of everyone and that we wouldn't have to worry about anything. He had a growth mindset and strived to position himself as well as those he loved in a better situation. He didn't see any limits to what was possible and felt very strong that he could achieve whatever he wanted.

Everyone who knew us knew we didn't play about Dante. Even

Dante's friends knew we didn't play about him and would definitely reach out to us when needed. My cousins would always joke and bring up how protective I was of him, especially when he was younger. I would often let them know if something happens to my brother, I'm going to hurt all of you. Dante was a very active child; he would run off without thinking about safety. He loved climbing, playing outside, riding his bike and playing sports. When he was younger, I would teach him how to fight because in my mind, my brother was not going to be a punk, and no one was going to walk over him. So, of course, I'm sure you would probably guess what happened-he loved to play fight and for some reason would end up in fights. No lie, I taught him well because he could throw some hands. Ok-that was the immature version of me. Because of his love for fighting and energy, when he was in high school, we enrolled him into boxing. He loved it. Truth be told, he would have gone far in boxing because of his skills and just love for the sport but my parents were not too fond of the sport.

The months leading up to his transition, we had the opportunity to help him get a truck to start a business. This is something he'd always dreamed of, having a truck. He just loved the idea of the size and sitting up high. It took some time, but we finally developed the business and called the business, Brothers with Tools. The business would offer landscaping, moving, hauling and just a variety of things. Our goal for the business was to be able to shine light on young African American men in a positive way by providing them with job opportunities that they may not normally have, offering them skills, and showing them a better way of making money. We were able to get him equipment and some jobs lined up. We also had family and friends who supported him. He was really handy and didn't mind getting his hands dirty at all. I remember while we were preparing for my daughter's Sweet 16 birthday celebration, and we were trying to get our yard more presentable for the party. My brother cleaned our yard to the point that it looked brand new. Every time I look at my backyard,

Lasting Impact

I think about my brother and all the hard work he (and his two assistants) did effortlessly. He took on the leadership role and ran the entire project. Once the backyard project was complete, we gave him the money to pay himself and the assistants. We told him "This is for you, and this is for them." My brother, who is selfless when it comes to looking out for others, gave his assistants some of his cut. When I asked him about it, his response was, "They did more than me sis and they worked so hard". My brother was the person that would take his shirt off his back and give it to someone else. He was always willing to help and lend a hand.

He was truly a light and the life of the party. His smile would light up any room. He found joy in bringing people together-having a family game night, cousin sleepovers and bowling tournaments. Let's not forget going out to eat; he loved going to the buffet. Whether it was the Asian buffet to get his favorite coconut shrimp or the good ole Old Country Buffet. At home, his favorite meals that I often made were my famous lasagna and seafood alfredo. We all knew not to leave any leftovers in the refrigerator we planned to eat later because he would eat them. Now sometimes he would ask but there were times when we would go in the refrigerator to warm our leftovers up and he already ate them.

The memories are endless and what helps me at times have peace and comfort during hard seasons. I often just sit and laugh thinking about our times together. On one of our many traveling adventures when Dante was a teenager, I believe like early middle school. we went on a vacation to Fort Lauderdale. We spent one night in Miami to give the older kids a South Beach experience. My husband and I were clueless at the time that South Beach had topless beaches, so we were walking and trying to find a spot on the beach. We start to notice the boys (Dante and my husband's brother, Alex) mouth wide open. There were women walking by who were topless and the boys' eyes were wide open. We couldn't help but laugh and run to cover our than 2-year old's eyes that happened to be wondering.

It was always an adventure during the summer months at the Cole house! My house was the house where the cousins and our brother's friends would come often. It was almost like we were running our own summer camp. They would spend the entire night playing video games, only to wake up playing the video games. They were the first in line before the neighborhood pool opened, and sometimes the last to leave. Dante and Alex would get so tanned from being in the sun all day at the pool. The lifeguards knew them well and they even made friends in the neighborhood. Their friends would knock on the door and ask if they could hang out with them. Dante loved being outside-from riding his bike all around the neighborhood we grew up in, to driving his car up and down the beltway as a young adult. I can remember our many car rides with him playing my favorite music and being so shocked when my daughter would know a song he played. I remember the many game nights we had at our house, and how he always loved to get everyone together for a good time.

Like I said, endless memories and there was never a dull moment in the life of Dante. His love, his smile, and his light we will cherish forever. His name will never be silenced and everyone who meets us will meet him. He impacted many and the impact will forever live on. Cherish the moments you have with the people you love. Take advantage of every moment and be very present. Do not allow the busyness of the world to stop you from spending time and creating memories with those you love. And most definitely do not let anger or unforgiveness stop you from creating more memories with the people you love. Tomorrow is not promised, neither is today. Make the most out of every moment. Because one day that moment will stand still.

Cherishing Memories, Creating Legacy

Memories are bridges between yesterday and tomorrow. While we can't make new ones with those we've lost, we can keep their spirit alive through intentional remembrance and meaningful action. Create your own memory treasury - a special box or digital collection filled with photos, messages, and mementos that tell their story. Write down the small moments that made them uniquely them, like their infectious laugh or the way they always knew exactly what to say.

Make memory-sharing a natural part of family gatherings. Let stories flow freely, beginning with "Remember when..." Record these precious conversations - future generations will treasure hearing their loved ones' voices sharing these memories. Most importantly, honor them through how you live. Support the causes that lit up their hearts. Continue the traditions that brought them joy. When facing decisions, let their values guide you.

Unbroken Key Takeaways

- The memories we create with loved ones are invaluable. They bring comfort, joy, and a reminder of the deep bonds we share.

- Being present in the lives of our loved ones creates lasting moments that can never be taken away. Showing up, supporting, and making time for family matters.

- Whether through laughter, shared traditions, tough conversations, or acts of service, love is not always spoken— it's lived out.

Unbroken Reflection Questions

- What are some of your most cherished memories with a loved one? How do those memories shape the way you view relationships today?

- How do you prioritize making time for your loved ones? Are there ways you can be more intentional in creating lasting memories?

- How do you express love and support to those in your life?

- If you could tell one person in your life how much they mean to you, who would it be, and what would you say?

CHAPTER FIVE

Making The Pain Less

"And we know that God causes everything to work together for the good of those who love God and are called according to his purpose for them."

Romans 8:28 (NLT)

From Disbelief to Purpose

From the time my mother's friend echoed what the doctor said, "they did all that they could", I was a little bit in disbelief because I had so much confidence that God was going to turn it around and my brother would leave the hospital with a mighty testimony. I was not prepared to, nor did I ever imagine hearing those words. In a split of a second, I went from unbelief to, "OK God, how are you going to turn this around for a girl? What is the purpose in this? How are you going to use me? How are you going to turn this around for good? Like, how can you make anything better than this with my brother no longer being here". I started to process all my different emotions and started wondering how God was going to use me for His purpose. This was the only thing that could possibly numb this instance of pain I was feeling, putting my hope in God's plan and knowing He will make this work for our good.

Many different emotions went through my mind that day and the days that followed. I would think to myself, "What if I would've just called him when my sister called me to try to talk to him? What if I just would've done that? What if I just would've reached out to him early enough in the day to ask him to come to the house before he went to my mom's house? What if I would've just done something different? What if…". Some many unanswered questions leading me right into a rabbit hole. I would go back and forth with thinking about the "what ifs" one moment and focusing on purpose the next. I often had to remind myself that he's gone; that he's no longer here for the things that I would have to say or could have done. There was nothing I could do at that moment that would change the outcome, which was one of the hardest things I had to realize. I had to learn to focus on the things that I could still control, and not on the things completely out of my control.

The Unprepared Journey

Grief, loss and death! Who really teaches you how to cope before it happens? Let's think about it. If you think about birth, there is so much preparation, conversations, and shared experiences. But grief, loss and death…nothing! We know it happens. We hope it never happens but there is no work done to prepare us in advance. The work doesn't start until it slaps us right in the face. I cannot remember being taught how to process and cope with death. Even watching others cope with the passing of a loved one, you never fully understand how to process or cope. I understood that one day we all must die but of course, I was thinking more like when we are all old and gray. I was not prepared to bury my brother, my younger brother, who was murdered by the person who he loved and was supposed to love him. No one has ever taught me how to process or cope with unexpected or premature loss. This was a new journey for me. In my mind, my brother would always be around. I mean, he was younger than me, so I never imagined burying him. I only imagine him having a successful business, getting married, and having kids. I would get so excited at the thought of attending his wedding and welcoming a niece, and/or nephew into the world one day. Thinking about all the things that were yet to come but now will never happen. All the things he would never get to experience and that I would never get to experience with him in his life, are so heartbreaking. Everything that I imagined happening one day will just be that-my imagination, and never my reality. This was hard to process, especially with watching others do exactly what I imagined experiencing with my brother in the future. There were times when it was hard for me to celebrate others and be happy for them because all I could think about was what I was missing out on. For a while it was hard for me to even talk to his friends as all I would think is my brother should be there and talking to them was another reminder of what I was missing out on because he was no longer here. This way of thinking was not making things better or making me feel any better. I had to change my thinking and how I was processing my emotions. I had to learn how to live in my new reality and realize that life was never going to be the same.

Finding New Ways Forward

I learned to focus on what made me smile, laugh and the things to be grateful for. I started to focus on what was still possible. I may not be able to experience certain things with my brother, but it didn't mean I couldn't still experience similar things. I could still celebrate with others and play a new role in the lives of others who needed a BIG SISTER. Yes, I would have preferred to have those experiences with Dante, but I couldn't lose sight of the experiences and memories we shared together while he was here-the family vacations, holidays, birthdays, special events at school and so much more. I had so many great memories to hold on to in my mind and in pictures. Every time I think about my brother, I just see him smiling and laughing. My memories of my brother are what I hold closest to me. His loving heart, infectious smile, and selflessness are something that cannot be denied. He lived a short life, but he lived a good life. His life was taken early but his life made an impact on the world. And now his story will change the world and save lives. These thoughts alone help lessen the pain. It helps me see the brighter side of things.

Processing Unexpected Loss

You may not have been taught how to effectively cope and process your emotions when it comes to grief. We understand that one day we will die but no one truly prepares us for losing someone close to our heart, especially a young person so suddenly and brutally. Losing a younger loved one truly throws your life for a loop and out of order. We are somewhat prepared for an older parent or loved one dying. We may not be ready, but we understand it's the order of things. But when a younger loved one, especially a sibling passes, it really messes up your mind. The way he was murdered by someone who supposedly loved him really messed me up mentally. He was taken away before it was his time. He still had much more life to live and impact to make. But someone decided to take matters into her own hands and steal his time away from him. This was a lot more to process than just a loved one passing. He was violently taken from us before his time.

Grief is complex, and it doesn't come with a manual. Everyone's experience is different, and there's no right or wrong way to feel. But there are healthy and unhealthy ways to cope, and recognizing the difference is crucial for your healing journey. Healthy coping skills are those that allow you to move through your grief instead of getting stuck in it, giving you the tools to navigate the ups and downs without losing yourself completely in the darkness. These skills are like lifelines-they won't take the pain away, but they can help you carry it in a way that doesn't destroy you.

Healthy vs. Unhealthy Coping

Healthy coping might look like leaning heavily on your faith, finding strength and comfort in prayer, or seeking guidance from a higher power. It could mean talking to a therapist who understands the layers of grief, joining a support group where you realize you're not alone, or journaling your emotions-getting the pain out of your head and onto paper. These are ways that help you process what you're going through, ways that give you space to feel everything without feeling like you're drowning. They help you begin to see that, although life will never be the same, there can still be good days, moments of joy, and moments of peace.

For me, I knew I was starting to heal when I found myself smiling again-genuinely smiling, not just forcing it to get through a conversation. When I was able to get out of bed, make a cup of coffee, and face the day without feeling like the weight of the world was sitting on my chest. It's not about rushing back to the life you had before, because the truth is. that life is gone. You're creating a new normal, a new way of living without your loved one, and that takes time-sometimes a lot of time. It's not about moving quickly; it's about moving at your own pace, taking it day by day, and even moment by moment when needed. Some days, the goal is just getting out of bed, and that's okay. Celebrate those small wins. Recognize the effort it took to smile, to laugh, to respond to a friend's text, to engage in a conversation without your mind drifting back to the why's and how's. And when you do, give yourself grace. Understand that healing doesn't mean you're forgetting; it doesn't mean the pain is gone forever. It just means you're learning to live with it, finding ways to carry it without letting it consume you. Healing is not a straight line, and definitely not a sprint. Some days, you'll feel like you're making progress, and then, out of nowhere, you'll have a bad day that knocks you off your feet. That's okay. It's part of the process. The important thing is that you don't give up on yourself, on life, or on the belief that there can be joy again, even in the midst of sorrow.

But just as there are healthy ways to cope, there are also unhealthy ways that might seem appealing, especially in those early, raw stages of grief when all you want is to numb the pain or make it go away. Turning to alcohol or drugs to dull the ache, isolating yourself from the people who care about you, neglecting your responsibilities, or feeling like life isn't worth living anymore-these are all signs that you're not managing your grief; you're running from it. It's so tempting to find an escape, to do anything that will provide some kind of relief, even if it's only for a few hours. You might feel that anger and vengeance are the answer, especially if your loved one's death was violent or unjust. In those moments, it feels like the only way to cope is to lash out, to find someone to blame, to make someone else hurt the way you're hurting. But all of that is just a temporary fix, a distraction from the deep, underlying pain that's still there. Unhealthy coping mechanisms are like numbing cream-they dull the pain for a little while, but it always comes back, and usually even stronger than before. They don't heal the wound; they just cover it up, and underneath, it's still festering. And the side effects of those choices can be devastating-not just for you, but for the people who love you and are walking this grief journey with you. They lead to more pain, more regret, and often, more grief. It's like trying to outrun a storm instead of learning how to weather it. The storm is going to come, no matter what you do. The key is to learn how to stand in the rain without letting it destroy you.

Healthy coping is not about eliminating the pain. That's impossible. It's about learning how to manage it, how to carry it without letting it crush you. It's about acknowledging that your life has changed forever, that the person you lost is not coming back, and that you're now living in a new reality-a reality where the memories, the pictures, and the moments you shared are all you have left. It's incredibly painful to accept, but it's also the first step toward healing.

The truth is you will never "get over" the loss. That's not the goal. You don't move on from grief; you move forward with it. It becomes a part of you, something you carry with you, but it doesn't have to be something that weighs you down forever. It's about finding ways to honor your loved one's memory, to keep them alive in your heart without letting the pain of their absence steal all your joy. You create new routines, new traditions, and find new ways to bring them into your everyday life. You learn that it's okay to be happy again, that laughter is not a betrayal of their memory. You allow yourself to feel joy without guilt, and you remember that your loved one would want you to live-not just to exist, but to truly live in this new reality. There will always be hard days, days when the grief hits you out of nowhere, and that's okay too. It's all part of the journey.

Ultimately, coping with grief in a healthy way means giving yourself permission to feel everything-the anger, the sadness, the joy, the love, and even the moments of relief. It's about creating a life that honors the person you lost without letting their absence define you. It's about finding beauty in the brokenness, about carrying your grief with grace, and about realizing that while the pain may never fully go away, you can find a way to live again, one step at a time.

Individual Paths Through Grief

It's important to understand that everyone may process loss differently, even those in the same family. You cannot compare your grief journey to another person's. You are not responsible for another person's grief; you are only responsible for your own grief journey. On this journey, it's important to allow yourself to process your emotions. It is not healthy for you to try to run or hide how you are feeling. I know sometimes it may feel that running or ignoring certain emotions will feel better than allowing yourself to feel them. I know it's easy to run because the pain is so heavy and you want to avoid or ignore it, but avoiding your feelings will only make the pain worse. The pain may never fully go away but you will begin to feel more peace and joy once you start to process your emotions. Learning to allow yourself to feel every emotion, can help lessen the pain. When you do not allow yourself to feel the emotions, it just continues to build up on the inside, which can lead to physical and mental health problems. Holding on to the pain is not going to bring your loved one back. It's only going to prevent you from living the life you still have or being there for the loved ones who are still alive. Unresolved pain causes more harm. We are not able to see people or situations for what they really are, and it causes us to build up hard walls around our hearts. Let's be honest, wouldn't your loved one want you to spend the time you have here on the earth living your life to the fullest? Would they want you to be unhappy all the time?

You must figure out what coping skills are beneficial to you on your grief journey. What may work for someone else, may not work for you. Be patient and kind to yourself as you find the best coping skills. Remember-do not let anyone tell you what will or will not work for you. You know yourself best. Dig deep and find what makes your soul happy. Find what helps to keep you in a state of peace when you're thinking or reminded of your loved one.

Creating Your Grief Plan

I've found it helps to have a grief plan. This is something you can have written or just in your mind, but I definitely recommend writing it down. In this plan, you will list the things that trigger your grief, what it feels like when you experience that trigger, what helps you when you're down, identify your negative coping skills, develop positive coping skills to replace the negative, who you can call on and when they should check on you. It's important to share this plan with the people who you believe you can call on, so they know when they need to lean in more towards you. This plan always helps you to prepare for the low moments and come out of them faster.

What can you do when you're feeling heaviness from the passing of your loved one? Remember, the journey through grief isn't about forgetting or "getting over" your loss - it's about learning to carry your memories with grace while continuing to live. Your path won't look like anyone else's, and that's okay. Take each day as it comes, be gentle with yourself as you navigate this new reality.

When the weight feels too heavy, return to your grief plan. Reach out to your support system. Most importantly, give yourself permission to feel whatever emotions arise. Your loved one would want you to find joy again, even while honoring their memory.

Unbroken Key Takeaways

- Even in deep loss, trusting that God will work things for good helps in the healing process.

- Focusing on "what ifs" can lead to a cycle of guilt and regret, but choosing to focus on what is still possible brings healing.

- Finding faith, therapy, support, and outlets for emotions can help process grief in a way that fosters healing rather than being stuck in pain.

- Healing takes time, and small victories matter. Smiling again, engaging in life, and embracing a new normal are signs of growth, not forgetting.

Unbroken Reflection Questions

1. In what ways have you seen God bring purpose from a painful situation in your life?

2. Are there any "what ifs" in your grief journey that you need to let go of?

3. How do you typically cope with loss? Are there any unhealthy habits you need to replace with healthier ones?

4. What small victories have you experienced in your healing journey, and how can you celebrate them?

5. What steps can you take today to continue moving forward while honoring your loved one's memory?

CHAPTER SIX

Moving Through Grief With Family

"All praise to God, the Father of our Lord Jesus Christ. God is our merciful Father and the source of all comfort.

He comforts us in all our troubles so that we can comfort others. When they are troubled, we will be able to give them the same comfort God has given us."

2 Corinthians 1:3-4 (NLT)

The First Night

Being the older sister, it's natural for me to check in on everyone else and make sure they are all okay. Most of the time this leads to me ignoring my own feelings and understanding and focusing on how other people feel.

Where do we go from here? How do we continue to live without him present? People were expecting him to live, to be okay and to walk out of that hospital. Friends and family members called me while we were at the hospital (and the following day) to check on his progress. They had been praying and hoping for a favorable outcome. "He didn't make it", were the words that tumbled out of my mouth. I hadn't even fully processed that fact that I had to tell my kids. They were unaware of what had happened and that we were at the hospital.

Breaking the News to the Children

Having to be the one to tell my kids, especially my daughter who had a close relationship with my brother, that he didn't make it was no easy conversation. They have been side-by-side since the day that she was born. She looked up to him; she counted on him. We decided to wait until the morning to tell them as by the time we got home we were drained, and it was late.

We weren't sure what to do after leaving the hospital since my parents and sister couldn't go back to their home, as the crime scene was still unclean. The house wasn't clean, so we had to figure something out. Should they go to a hotel? A family member's house? What about my brother's dog who stayed at my parent's house and was still at the house in her crate. My husband spoke up and said everyone should just come to our house, which was such a relief because we were not thinking clearly. He even said my brother's dog could come too. I was shocked as he is not a huge fan of dogs. We said goodnight to our family and friends who were gathering with us at the hospital and followed each other to my parents' house for them to grab some things and get the dog.

While driving to my parents' house, I was in the car alone, my thoughts were everywhere, and I was in disbelief of everything that just transpired. I was thinking the doctors made a mistake. Did they do all that they could? I mean he's an African American male, it's possible, right? I literally felt like I was dreaming and the words to describe that moment still are unfound.

When we arrived at the house, I couldn't go in. I don't understand how any of them went into the house-my dad, my sister, her boyfriend. My mom stayed outside the house. They went to the house, and they got their stuff. My sister went to her boyfriend's house, while my mom and dad came to my house. I had to go home to be with my kids. I wasn't ready to face them or tell them. On the way to the house, we just called them to let them know that something was going on at Papa and Grandma's house and that they had to come stay at our house that night. But I knew that the time was going to come in the morning when I would have to tell them as friends and family members would be coming to the house.

I was able to get some sleep that night, which I found surprising because of all of the questions that I had, a little bit of disbelief that I had, and the internal emotional storm I was feeling. But I also had this sense of peace; maybe it was a shock. Expectantly, people started filling my house the next morning, some even before I was fully awake. We couldn't wait any longer, the time was now where we had to tell our kids. The hardest part of grieving someone that you love and/or are close with is processing your emotions and coming to the reality that they are now gone. Another hard part is telling those that you love that they are no longer here, especially young kids. At the time my daughter was 16 and my sons were 11 and 6. My husband has always said that I always know the right words to say, so he had me to lead the conversation. My heart dropped as I explained that their uncle was no longer here. "No no, no, not Dante, not Dante". My oldest son yelled out a cry for his uncle while my daughter cried hysterically. My youngest son may have been too young to process such a tragedy at this point in his life, but I'm sure he felt something. He just ran out of the room. The following days were hard on my daughter. There were times when she almost passed out, had a hard time breathing and her body got stiff. My husband and I constantly reminded her to breathe and assured her that it was okay to cry, be mad and express her pain. Our family continued to wrap their hands around her and just sat with her. I would often find her just sitting and staring off into the distance. It was challenging watching my kids experience such grief as I was learning to navigate my own. I did not have the answers and sometimes not even the words. All I could say, and think was, "God got us, He will see us through."

I spoke to my sister, and she really didn't get much sleep and of course she was very emotional. I told her to come to the house so we could be together. As she arrived, she found me right away and we hugged and didn't let go. It was only us now, our little brother-our heart, our everything-had been taken from us. All I could do at that moment was play the song, "Father, can you hear me", from the Tyler Perry movie, *Diary of a Mad Black Woman*. We needed his presence. The pain was too much.

That same day while emotions were still extremely high, the family of my brother's girlfriend had no knowledge of what happened. During their search for his girlfriend, they called my daughter's phone to inquire about her whereabouts as she wasn't answering her phone, nor did she make it home. They had no idea their loved one was in jail, and my brother passed away. My sister was the one who answered the phone when the family called, and she spared no detail when it came to expressing herself and sharing the devastating news. At that moment, reality set in and the journey to live life without Dante became so real.

The Ripple Effect of Loss

I felt so bad during this whole process for my sister's boyfriend and my dad. They witnessed everything that happened on August 12, 2020, and they carried so much guilt around the incident that happened that day. Every time someone would ask them what happened, they had to relive that day over, and over, and over again. I'm sure they replayed every moment even when they weren't talking to others about it. People would just ask them questions that are also very unfair to them like, "Why didn't you do this? Why did you do that?" To me that was very unfair and inconsiderate. Going to the grieving process is already hard but having to witness the passing of a loved one I'm sure would intensify the whole process. They were already asking themselves questions like, "What could I have done different? How did I miss certain things? How did she get the knife from the kitchen without me seeing? How come I didn't see what was actually in her hand?" People offered their own opinion and what they would have done in the situation. But if we are honest, you don't know what you would really do if you were in the situation. My dad, we believe, went into shock. My sister and I were on the phone with him after everything happened and he was not coherent at all. He continued to just repeat himself when asked a question or give an unrelated response to our questions.

Paul, my husband, had a very hard time with Dante's passing. As the rock of our family, Paul tried his best to be strong for me and the kids. He stepped into the role of protector, ensuring we were all okay, but in the process, he neglected his own grief. He was so focused on supporting us and making sure we had what we needed that he didn't take the time to process his own pain. Paul was a man of action-always taking care of others-so much so that he put his own heartache on the back burner.

There was one night, though, when everything caught up with him, and he broke down. I had been so consumed with my own grief; I hadn't checked in on him. I had become so wrapped up in my own pain that I didn't realize I had neglected him. Paul had lost someone too; someone he loved deeply. Dante was not just my brother—he was someone Paul cared for, someone who was a big part of his life, and in many ways, Paul had played an important role in raising him. Dante saw him as a father figure, and that bond was irreplaceable.

I had to take a step back and recognize that Paul was grieving in his own way, and his pain was just as real as mine. He had always been there for Dante, always supportive, always guiding him. And now, in the silence of his grief, I realized that Paul was just as lost as I was. He kept saying over and over again, "Not Dante. Why did this happen to him? He should still be here." I knew those words came from a deep place of hurt and disbelief. The reality of Dante's death felt just as unfair to Paul as it did to the rest of us. It was senseless. Dante was so full of life, so full of potential, and losing him was a wound that no one in our family could have prepared for. It was in that moment when I truly understood that grief affects everyone differently, and just because someone seems like they're holding it together, doesn't mean they aren't falling apart on the inside. Paul had been strong for so long, for all of us, that when it finally hit him, it was overwhelming. I had to remind myself to check in on him, to be there for him just as he had been for me. I couldn't let his grief go unnoticed.

We both carried the weight of this loss in different ways, but what kept us strong was our ability to lean on each other. It wasn't easy, but we learned to share our pain, to grieve together, and to allow ourselves the space to hurt. Paul and I both had to face the fact that losing Dante changed us, but it also strengthened our bond. Grief doesn't just affect individuals-it affects families. It affects relationships, and if you don't communicate through it, it can leave you disconnected. But through it all, we had each other to lean on, even in those quiet moments when words were too hard to find. Paul misses Dante in ways I can't even express; and I miss Dante in ways Paul may never be able to express.

Amaya, my daughter, had an incredibly hard time dealing with Dante's passing- and honestly, even to this day, it still affects her eminently. Losing her uncle was like losing a piece of herself, and her grief manifested in ways that were hard for me to watch as a mother.

She loved Dante so much-he was her riding partner, her playmate, her confidant-and losing him left an ache in her heart that was ineffable.

Recognizing that she needed guidance with her grief, I made sure to get her into grief therapy around the same time I started mine. We both knew that it was essential for her to have a space where she could express her pain and try to navigate through the emotions she couldn't always understand or manage. Even though she was young, the grief was just as heavy for her as it was for the rest of us. It affected everything—her mood, her focus, and even her grades. At first, I didn't realize how much it was impacting her schoolwork until I started to see the signs. Her once bright and motivated spirit seemed clouded by sadness, and I knew I needed to step in to make sure she had the support she needed.

Things worsened when schools reopened after COVID-19, and she had to face the reality of seeing Dante's girlfriend's sister at school. It triggered something deep inside her, and she had multiple panic attacks over the next few weeks back in school. The first time it happened, I rushed to her side. I knew it wasn't just about the encounter-it was everything that Dante's death had left unspoken and unresolved inside her. Over time, it happened again, and then again. That's when I reached out to the school counselor, desperate to find a solution. We worked together to develop a plan that would keep Amaya from seeing her at school, at least for a while. They made sure she wouldn't share any classes with the girl, and they even rearranged her schedule so that they wouldn't cross paths in the hallways.

Even though we worked hard to create some space for her to heal, I can see that Amaya still struggles with her grief. It's not something that just "gets better" over time for her. Every now and then, I see the pain in her eyes, and I know it's a part of her that will never fully heal.

She misses her uncle beyond what words can convey. There were times when she would get so quiet, lost in her thoughts, and I'd find myself wondering if she was asking the same questions I was: "Why did this happen? Why is Dante not here with us?"

I'm thankful that Amaya has started to find healing in her own way. Her therapy sessions have helped her process, and she's learning to take it day by day. But I know it's going to take time. She's still a young soul, and she loved her uncle with such a pure heart. The void that his passing left in her life will always be there, and all I can do is continue to guide her through it, make sure she knows it's okay to grieve, and be there for her as she navigates the waves of emotion. I remind her often that it's okay to miss him, and it's okay to feel all of it-the sadness, the anger, the confusion. But one thing I'm sure of is that she'll carry his love with her. Just like the rest of us, she'll always carry a piece of Dante in her heart, and that's something no one can ever take away.

I wanted to take everyone's pain away, but the grief therapist gave me the best advice. She said, "You are only responsible for your grief. You cannot grieve for other people. You cannot take their pain away. You can pray for them and be there for them. But do not try to take on their grief." My family has always been close, but this truly brought us closer. For the first time in years, we were living under the same roof. The only way to get through this was for us to draw close together and lean on each other. Exactly what Dante would want us to do. I often thought about how happy he would be if he could see all of us together, family coming from near and far. He was always all about family and would always try to bring everyone together as one.

My sister had a really hard time coping with Dante's passing. She and Dante were close in age, and they shared a unique bond, one that was filled with laughter, inside jokes, and a deep understanding of each other. They were more than siblings—they were best friends. I know she felt the weight of losing him in a way that was hard for anyone to truly grasp unless they'd experienced that kind of closeness. As for me, Dante and I were incredibly close as well, but to watch my sister grieve the loss of someone she had grown up with, someone who had been a constant in her life, was heartbreaking. Our trio of siblings—Dante, my sister, and I—was now broken, and it felt like a part of our foundation had crumbled. In the weeks that followed the funeral, we fell apart. The grief hit us differently, and instead of leaning on each other, we found ourselves pulling away. We didn't talk for months. It was like we couldn't find the words, the comfort, or the strength to bridge the distance that had come between us. I thought we'd never be able to get back to where we were before. The pain was too raw, and the weight of the loss was too much to bear. But God!

God always has a plan, even when we can't see it. Even when things seem hopeless, He is working behind the scenes, bringing healing where there is hurt and light where there is darkness. Through all of our pain and confusion, God was orchestrating a reunion that would bring us back together. We began talking again, slowly at first, but eventually, we found our way back to each other. What the enemy meant for evil, God is turning into something good. He's using our hurt to rebuild our bond, and I am so thankful for that. We are closer than ever now, and though we'll never fully understand why Dante's life was taken so soon, we trust that God is using this experience to shape us, to teach us, and to remind us of His grace. The enemy tried to tear us apart, but God is restoring us, and I truly believe that in the end, we are stronger because of it. We are not just surviving this loss-we are learning to live with it, together, as a family. With God at the center of it all, I know we will continue to heal and grow, even in the midst of the pain.

As time has passed, we continue to move through grief together, taking it one day at a time, doing our best to support one another. We've learned that being present for each other doesn't always mean having the right words to say—it's just showing up, being there, and allowing each other to feel and heal at our own pace. We've found comfort in one another's company, and although the pain is still there, we lean on our family in ways we never have before.

Everyone has slowly started to return to their routines. My parents, despite the heavy weight of their grief, have been able to return to the house. It's been a long road for them, but they're showing up, one step at a time. For me, it took longer to return to their house-the place where my brother's life was taken from him. I couldn't bring myself to go inside for a long time, but I started by just being in the yard-even that felt like a big step. The memories linger there, both painful and beautiful, but it was important for me to reconnect with that space, to reclaim it in a way that felt right. It's funny how my oldest son reminds me and my sister so much of Dante. His smile, the way he moves through the world-it's almost as if Dante is still with us in the little moments. That's been a beautiful and bittersweet thing.

Even in the midst of moments that remind us of Dante, there are still days when the grief is so heavy, it's hard to breathe. My mom, especially. She has a blank stare at times, and I can tell she's trying to hold it together. I can feel her pain, even when she doesn't say anything. She's been so strong for us, but I know that losing Dante has completely rocked her world. She's such an integral part of our lives, and her strength in the face of this loss is both heartbreaking and inspiring.

My dad, too, has his own way of dealing with it. He's more quiet about his hurt, but every now and then, he'll open up to my sister, letting her in on what he's feeling. It's not often but when it happens, it feels like a breakthrough. He has always been someone who keeps things close to the chest. I know this pain, though silent, runs deep for him as well.

Through it all, I continue to pray for my family. I thank God for keeping us together, for providing strength even when we feel so weak. He's seen us through every dark moment, and I know that even in the midst of the pain, we've been blessed with unity. We miss Dante every single day. His absence has left an indescribable void in our hearts, but we carry his memory with us. We find strength in one another, and while the pain may never fully leave, we know we have each other, and that's a blessing we don't take for granted.

Grief has a way of amplifying everything—the pain, the loss, the little things we wouldn't normally think twice about. It puts a strain on every relationship, and it's so easy to let that pain turn into anger or frustration, especially when you're around the people who are hurting just as much as you are. But during times like this, it's so important to remember that grief doesn't only affect you. Your family members are all dealing with the same loss, just in different ways. They might not handle it the way you do, and that's okay. It's crucial to give each other the space to grieve in their own way, even if it doesn't look like what you expect or want. Be gentle, be kind, and give each other grace.

When you're grieving, emotions are raw. Things that might not normally bother you can suddenly feel unbearable, and words spoken in the heat of grief can cut much deeper. There were times when my family and I weren't seeing eye to eye, and tensions were high. In those moments, I had to remind myself that we were all trying to navigate this pain together. It's not about winning an argument or proving a point-it's about sticking together, even when it's hard. If you have to take a deep breath and step away for a moment, that's okay. Sometimes you need a pause to collect yourself, to choose your words carefully, and to respond with compassion instead of frustration. It's about finding a way to respond with love, even when you're feeling hurt. I'm not saying you should accept mistreatment or pretend that everything is fine when it's not. Boundaries are still important, even in grief. But grace doesn't mean ignoring how you feel—it means choosing to approach your family with understanding, choosing to see them through the lens of compassion rather than judgment. It's about giving each other the benefit of the doubt because everyone's heart is heavy. Some days, you have to be the strong one, even when you don't feel strong at all, because you know that unity is so much more important than being right.

Grief has this way of making us all so vulnerable, exposing the cracks in our relationships that maybe we didn't even know were there. But instead of letting those cracks break us, we can use this time to come together, to be each other's safe haven in the storm. Disagreements will happen, tempers will flare, but don't let those moments define your family. If anything, grief should remind us how precious time is—how we can't afford to let petty arguments and misunderstandings tear us apart. It's not the time to point fingers or dig up old wounds. It's a time to link arms, to draw closer, and to find strength in each other when you feel like you have none left.

The Power of Prayer and Unity

One of the most powerful things we did as a family was to pray together. In those moments, I could feel a shift. I could feel the kind of peace that only comes from connecting with God and each other. Praying together was a way to lay it all down, to acknowledge that we didn't have all the answers, and to seek strength beyond ourselves.

There's something deeply healing about coming together in prayer, about lifting each other's burdens and trusting that God is with us, even in the darkest moments. It's a reminder that we don't have to carry this alone, that we have each other, and we have Him.

I also learned the importance of seeking therapy individually. Grief affects everyone differently, and sometimes, it's just too heavy to unpack in a group setting. Therapy gave me the tools to process my own pain, to sort through all the tangled emotions, and to heal in my own time. And when each of us took the time to heal individually, we could come back together as a family, a little more whole, a little more ready to support each other without dragging our own unresolved pain into every conversation. Therapy isn't about being weak-it's about finding strength in the midst of brokenness, so you can be the best version of yourself for the people you love.

I can't stress enough how important it is to give each other room to breathe. Grief is exhausting, and sometimes, your family might need space, not because they don't care, but because they're just trying to survive the weight of it all. Respect that space and know that it doesn't mean they don't love you. It means they're hurting too, and they're doing their best to cope in the way that makes the most sense to them. At the end of the day, it's about choosing to love each other through the mess of it all, to keep showing up for each other even when it's hard. Grief doesn't play fair, and it doesn't come with a rulebook, but if you can stick together, if you can choose love over anger and grace over judgment, you'll find a way through. It's not about forgetting or moving on-it's about holding onto each other while you carry the weight of the loss, knowing that together, you can bear what feels unbearable on your own.

And remember, while you can't change what happened to your loved one, you can use the strength of your family to ensure that their memory lives on in a way that brings light and healing to others. Grief, when handled together with love, can turn into something beautiful-something that transforms pain into purpose. Your family can be that beacon of hope for someone else. You have the power to turn the worst thing that ever happened into a story of resilience, strength, and love.

Unbroken Key Takeaways

- Everyone experiences grief differently, even within the same family. It is important to support each other while also respecting individual grief journeys.

- Grief can be delayed or hidden, and it's important for people to take the time to process their own emotions rather than focusing only on others.

Unbroken Reflection Questions

1. How do I support others in their grief while also tending to my own needs?

2. What steps can I take to be present for my loved ones while also making space for my own emotional journey?

3. How do I respond to others' grief in a way that is compassionate and non-judgmental?

4. Am I allowing myself the space to grieve fully?

5. How can I lean on my faith during times of loss and grief?

CHAPTER SEVEN

Me, Myself, And GRIEF

"The Lord is close to the brokenhearted; He rescues those whose spirits are crushed."

Psalm 34:18 (NLT)

The Initial Wave of Pain

G rief has brought an exorbitant amount of pain to me, it's a heartache that never leaves; a nightmare I can't wake up from. But God!

For the next few months, we had friends and family calling, texting, checking on us, bringing food by and stopping by the house. I wasn't in the right space to eat. How could I eat when my brother wasn't here to enjoy the food with me. How can I laugh when my brother isn't here to laugh with me. I had a hard time connecting with people. My thoughts were, "wow if this is what it feels like to lose someone that you love, I don't want to have to feel this feeling again'. I had a hard time processing such a moment of disbelief. People offered to help in any way they could. I just wanted someone to bring my brother back. I just needed God to bring my brother back.

My house was full, but I found myself feeling alone. I had no interest in entertaining guests, answering their questions, or addressing their concerns. I just wanted to be alone, I didn't want to talk to anyone outside of my immediate family. At that time, I wasn't ready for comments from outsiders, and felt some people were better off not speaking at all. It's important to foster a sense of presence and support for those who are grieving, offering them the comfort of being truly seen and heard; just let them know that you're there and care for them.

The Overwhelming Support

I was very grateful for all the support but even more grateful for the moments we shared hilarious memories and even the silent moments. Thank you, Lord, for the memories. The amount of love and support we received was just a constant reminder of how blessed we were and the impact my brother had on everyone.

Of course, after someone's transition, we have to plan the funeral. It was 2020, so we were still in the depth of COVID, and we still had government and state issued restrictions. Due to the fact that this was a murder case, we had to wait for the investigators to finish reviewing my brother's body and gathering their information before my brother could be transferred to the funeral home. Wow! Just to write the word *murder*, stings me to my core. We began the process of searching for a funeral home right away and coordinated with the police as to where to send the body. The next couple of weeks, we began planning a funeral, and I had to start the process of living life here on earth without Dante. Every day I would just look at my door and think of how he would come to the house and come in the garage door. I could visualize him walking through the door and saying "Sis, what are you doing sis?". Every day I knew he was going to walk in the door. I believed he was going to walk in the door again, but that day never came. That day wasn't going to come and all I wanted to do was sleep.

The Weight of Decision Making

Being the older sister, my family leaned on me with decision making and it was so difficult. I didn't want to talk about it, think about it or even decide on arrangements. I was still processing everything. I was still trying to figure out how to continue to live. When we had our first viewing of the body, once it was finally released to the funeral home, I couldn't even go into the room. I felt nude, I couldn't look. I couldn't see my baby brother laying in a casket, not talking or breathing. My family tried to help me get past my decision but every time I got close to the door, I couldn't move. From outside the room, I heard crying. I watched family members walk out of the room crying. I heard them say things like, "I can't believe this. She stabbed him so many times. What did all the scratches on his face and neck come from?' I wanted to see him. I wanted to hug him, but my body would not move. As days and weeks passed, we finalized the funeral arrangements, and it was time. It was time for us to celebrate and honor my brother's life. We asked everyone to wear white to honor Dante. There was an overflowing amount of love and support from family, friends and even strangers. The funeral home is at full capacity in the middle of COVID. The funeral was originally scheduled to be held at the gravesite but due to the rain we received that morning, we had to hold the funeral inside. Some people had to listen from outside of the funeral home as even the overflow rooms were full. This was the last time I would see my brother in his physical body. Just like the first viewing, I felt nude. I kept asking my family, do I have to go in? Everyone offered their encouragement in a gentle and understanding way, fully supporting me regardless of the decision I chose to make.

I DID IT YALL. I made it into the room and up to the casket. I was full of so many emotions. Dante was laying there looking so peaceful and just like he was sleeping. I kept touching him, praying that he would just get up; just open his eyes, walk out of here and end this nightmare. I couldn't stop looking at him, praying and hoping this was just a dream. Once the service started. I do not know what came over me, but I allowed God to take full control. He even sent me a message that needed to be heard. I spoke about my brother, forgiveness and cherishing your loved ones. Everything was perfect, from the singers to the tributes, all up to the eulogy. Everything was just perfect. When they came to close the casket, I had to leave the stand. I cannot stomach watching the casket close. I sat outside the room until it was done. My mom was so brave, she helped close the casket and stood up there during the whole process. As we moved to his gravesite it became harder and harder. I was full of so many different emotions. I was sad and angry because we were at a funeral for my brother, overjoyed by all the love and support, grateful for the times I shared with him and the impact he had on others on his short time here on earth, and hopeful for how God was going to use his story to change lives. I was so happy to see families who traveled near and far. Their presence meant so much.

There were so many moments that brought me joy and happy tears. It's like God knew what I needed and exactly when I needed it most. This one time, my six-year-old knew exactly what to say to help turn my mood around. I have no idea where this little one got his wisdom from, but he would remind me to focus on the memories. It's almost like he would listen to me and then regurgitate back. "Dante's in heaven. Now focus on the memories mom; he's always with us."

Finding Comfort in Dreams

In my mind I just felt like oh he's going to come and visit me in my dreams. I just kept asking God to please let me know that Dante is okay, please let me know that he's with you. It took months for him to appear in my dreams. I remember the first dream I had. We were out somewhere during a family outing as we did frequently. We were at a go-kart track (one of Dante's favorite places to go). We had a go-kart track within walking distance when we were younger, and he went there almost every day. In my dream, I had just finished a race, and I got out of my car to talk to someone. When I was about to get back in my car, I looked over and someone was sitting in my car. It was Dante. He was smiling and talking to other people. He wasn't looking at me and we didn't make eye contact, but he was talking to my kids and my husband. When I woke up, I knew he was okay and at peace. God had given me the sign I longed for, seeing my Dante's smile. The fact that he was sitting in my seat let me know that I could let go and live.

Preserving Memories Through Messages

I often sit and read over the text messages between Dante and me. These conversations mean so much to me, now more than ever. These texts weren't just words on a screen-they were moments of connection, love, and support that I now hold close to my heart. As you'll see below, they reflect not only the bond Dante and I shared but also the way he expressed his pride in me, his unwavering love, and how much he truly cared for the people in his life. These conversations remind me of the depth of our relationship and the encouragement we gave one another. Though I can no longer hear his voice or feel his presence, I find comfort in these messages, as they continue to serve as a reminder of the love we had. Looking back, it's clear to me now just how much he believed in me, and I will carry that with me for the rest of my life. I share these screenshots in hopes that they can serve as a reminder to cherish the relationships you have now. To express love and gratitude while you still can, because there's no greater gift than the words and moments we share with those we love.

Tha phone

Did you apologize

Yea I think so don't member

Omg you always start and end with an apology
Did she say anything or just hung up

Yea & did both

Did you try to text or call her back

Yea & we talk sum more she just upset

She has a ri t to
You was w ong

I kno

Wat movie y'all gonna go see & see if she wants 2 go

& don't be worryin bout tha t mobile plan I got that just enjoy your new watch 😈 u earned it

Dante

that was your lawnmower. You got it a long time ago. Pick it up when you ready

It's okay I did it already & I figured u was & thankx dad

Text Message • SMS
29 Mar 2020 at 3:45 PM

Call you back shortly

iMessage

Ight

30 Mar 2020 at 3:22 PM

Pause for a Purpose
youtu.be

30 Mar 2020 at 5:31 PM

Proud of you 🙌🤍

Text Message • SMS

It's hard to put into words just how much Dante's smile meant to me. He had this way of lighting up a room, of making everything feel a little bit lighter and brighter, even when it seemed like the weight of the world was pressing down. His smile was more than just an expression—it was a feeling; it was a warmth that could wrap around you and make your worst days feel like your best. It's the kind of smile that lingers; the kind you carry with you long after it's gone. Dante was a caretaker through and through. He had this beautiful, almost innocent desire to make sure everyone was okay. He'd often say things like, "I'm going to take care of everyone. I'm going to buy us all a house and set everyone up nicely." Those were his dreams, his way of showing love, and sometimes I wonder if, in his own way, he felt he had to go before us. Maybe he needed to get a head start, to make sure everything was in order, to start building a house in heaven, just like he said he would here on earth. Little did we know, he'd be watching over us from above, making sure we're okay in a different way. And every time I see the number 22, his age when he left us, I can't help but smile. It's like a little nod from him, a reminder that he's still here in his own way.

Learning to Live with Grief

For a long time, I couldn't go anywhere near my mother-in-love's house, as Dante's girlfriend lived in the same neighborhood. It was so hard to avoid as my kids went to school in that area and my mother-in-love lived there. My kids could no longer catch the bus home to their grandmother's house. We would have to pick them up directly from the school or send them to an after-school program. Her neighborhood became this painful reminder of what I'd lost, of the countless times I'd driven up to drop Dante off or pick him up, our conversations on the way there, and the way he'd wave goodbye. Just the thought of seeing that house, of facing those memories head-on, felt extremely heavy. I'd avoid the entire area, take a different route, and if I had no choice but to pass by, I'd keep my eyes straight ahead, refusing to even glance in the direction of the house. It was too much-too raw, too real, and overflowing with memories I wasn't ready to face.

Grief has a way of creeping up on you when you least expect it. It doesn't follow a timeline, and it doesn't let you plan for when it hits the hardest. There are days when it feels like a weight pressing down on my chest, and other days when it feels like a gentle whisper reminding me of all the love we shared. I've had to learn to navigate those ups and downs, to recognize and respect my triggers, and to give myself the grace to feel whatever I'm feeling without judgment. Some days, it's okay to cry. Some days, it's okay to laugh and smile at the memories. I'm learning that grief doesn't mean letting go-it means carrying my brother with me, in the good days and the bad.

Dante meant everything to me. His absence is a hole that can never truly be filled, and that's okay. I'm learning that missing him doesn't have to mean living in sadness. I know he'd want me to continue living, to find joy in the small moments, to laugh, to smile, and to enjoy life just as he did. I know he'd be proud of me for finding ways to tell his story, to honor his life, and to share the lessons I've learned with others. He'd want me to be strong, to keep moving forward, and to use my pain as a testimony to help others who might be going through the same thing.

This journey isn't easy, and it's not one I ever expected to be on. But I know that Dante is with me, guiding me, encouraging me to keep going. His spirit is still here, in the number 22 that seems to follow me, in the memories that make me laugh and cry, and in the love that continues to grow even though he's no longer physically here. I hold onto that love, because it's what gets me through the hard days and makes the good days even sweeter. One day at a time, I'm learning to carry him with me-not as a burden, but as a light that continues to shine, even in the darkest moments. I know he's smiling down, proud of how I've kept his memory alive, and that's all the encouragement I need to keep going. Grief has changed me, but it hasn't broken me. I'm still here, still living, still laughing, and still finding ways to honor the brother who meant the world to me. Because I know, deep down, that's what he would have wanted.

Finding Healing Through Writing

One way I learned to cope with the overwhelming pain of losing Dante was through journaling. It became my safe space, my quiet moment to release all the raw emotions I was carrying. The process of writing helped me organize the chaos in my mind, and through the ink on the page, I began to find clarity. Sometimes, the words didn't come out neatly or perfectly, but they always came. And one of the most healing things I did was write letters to Dante.

These letters became my conversation with him when I couldn't speak directly to him. I'd write as though he could hear me, as though he was sitting right there. I poured my heart out, sharing the pain, the memories, and the questions I still had. It gave me a sense of connection, even though he wasn't physically here anymore. Writing to him helped ease my soul in ways I can't explain. In these letters, I found my grief being validated—each word was a step towards healing. It became a release of all the things I didn't have the words to say in normal conversation. It gave me space to be honest with myself and with Dante. And while I'll never have the answers to all my questions, I know that through writing, I was able to move forward, piece by piece. This letter is one of those moments—where the words flowed from my heart to the page, an unfiltered expression of my grief, love, and longing.

A Letter to My Brother

Dear Dante,

I miss you so much not one single day goes by without me thinking about you. I wish you were here with us still. I wish you could see how much Charles and Bryce have grown. They remind me so much of you in so many ways. I wish I could tell you how much I love you. How much you mean to me. How much you helped me. I love you so much and appreciate you more than words can describe. You were always there when I needed; no questions asked. You always stepped in without even being asked. I hope you know how much you were loved. That you were perfect as you are. That you meant the world to so many people and how our lives will never be the same without you. I wish I had more time with you. More time to love you and to see you fully grow into everything God planned for you. I wish I could have saved you. I wish I could have shown you how much you were loved and appreciated. Dante, I promise I'm going to fight for you. I'm going to make sure your voice is not silenced, that people know you and remember you and are blessed by your life. I won't give up Dante. I'm going to continue to fight for you and others. I'm so grateful for all the memories we shared, and I hold them close. You meant the world to me and it's hard to live without you, but I know I have to fight for you. I have to fight. Love always, Marcia.

I encourage you, whether you're grieving the loss of a loved one or even just struggling with a difficult time in your life, to try writing a letter to that person. It doesn't have to be a perfect letter or even a formal one. Just let it flow. Write down everything you're feeling—your love, your frustration, your unanswered questions. Pour it all out on the page. In these letters, you'll find a safe space to grieve, to heal, and to reconnect in a way that brings comfort to your soul. Sometimes we need to let the words flow freely in order to release the weight that we carry. These letters may not bring answers, but they can help bring peace to your heart. And over time, they'll help you find a way to carry forward the love you have for your loved one, even when they're no longer physically present. Try it—you might be surprised by the comfort it brings and how it helps you process and heal. Grief doesn't have a set timeline, but writing those letters helped me find moments of peace, and I believe it can help you, too. Let your heart speak, let your grief unfold, and let the words be a part of your healing journey.

Unbroken Key Takeaways

- In moments of grief, sometimes words aren't enough. Just being present, offering silent support, and showing love can be more impactful than trying to offer solutions or advice.

- Saying a final goodbye can be very hard. It's okay to not be ready to make decisions or face certain moments, such as seeing them for the last time. Finding ways to honor their memory, like through a special funeral or a tribute, can bring both closure and comfort

- In the midst of profound loss, turning to God for comfort and clarity is vital. God offers peace, signs of assurance, and messages of hope, even when the pain seems insurmountable.

- The importance of expressing our love while people are still with us cannot be overstated—what remains are the messages, memories, and bonds we created.

Unbroken Reflection Questions

1. Have you experienced a moment in your grief where you felt overwhelmed by both the support around you and the loneliness inside? How did you navigate this tension?

2. How have you found comfort in the midst of your own losses? Are there specific memories or messages that have helped you heal?

3. In what ways can you show up for someone who is grieving? What is one simple thing you could do to support someone in their mourning?

4. What is one thing you could do today to show gratitude to the people you love and appreciate while they are still here? How can you express your love in a tangible way?

CHAPTER EIGHT

Negative Outcomes Of Domestic Violence

"Guard your heart above all else, for it determines the course of your life."

Proverbs 4:23 (NLT)

The Cycle of Abuse

It took me a long time to truly understand the kind of relationship my brother was in and how damaging it was for both of them. They had been off and on since high school, eventually reconnecting two years after graduation. From the beginning, something in my gut told me that she wasn't right for him. Maybe it was the protective older sister in me, but I knew they weren't compatible. She didn't bring out the best in my brother, and I had always hoped he'd find someone who would lift him up, not drag him down.

As time went on, it became clearer just how toxic their relationship really was. It wasn't just disagreements or arguments-it was verbal, emotional, and physical abuse from both sides. My brother would tell me stories when they were on a break. There were stories about how she acted and the things she'd say, and every time I'd be relieved that they were apart. But then, they'd reconnect, and I'd watch him get pulled back into that damaging cycle, unable to truly understand what was happening beneath the surface.

As an older sister, there's this deep instinct to protect. You want the best for your siblings; you want to see them with someone who appreciates their worth, who uplifts and supports them. You hope they find someone who makes them better, not someone who drains their spirit. She wasn't that person for him. She'd poke at him, taunt him, push his buttons just to see him lose his cool. It was as if seeing him frazzled and upset was a game to her-a form of twisted entertainment. And the worst part was, we only saw a fraction of what was really going on. We noticed how she would bait him, creating conflict over minor things, things that could have easily been avoided. It was like watching an older sibling torment a younger one, enjoying the chaos they could stir up. Yet, we never truly understood how deep the emotional manipulation ran. We didn't see the full extent of the emotional and verbal abuse she inflicted, or the slow, insidious way she chipped away at his confidence, the cruel words that left scars we couldn't see.

My brother was always such a hard worker, so willing to put in the effort to get things done. He was dependable, driven, and never afraid of a challenge. But during that relationship, I saw those qualities fade. He became stressed, unmotivated, and distant-like the light in him had dimmed. It wasn't just the stress of everyday life; it was something more profound, more damaging. He looked defeated, as if the weight of the world was pressing down on his shoulders, and he had no idea how to shake it off. I don't want to say she was the sole cause, but there's no doubt in my mind that she played a significant role in his decline.

These patterns weren't new; they had been there all along. But it wasn't until I started piecing together stories from the past that I fully realized how dangerous their relationship had become. I'll never forget hearing about the day she showed up at my brother's friend's house, looking for him. He wasn't there yet, as he was still at work, but his friend was home, and he opened the door to her. Without hesitation, she declared she was there to kill my brother, storming into the kitchen to search for a knife. His friend thought she was joking-brushed it off as an overreaction. But now, looking back, I realize those were not empty words. That moment, like so many others, was just another sign of how far-gone things had become. There were marks on my brother's body-scratches, bruises-and whenever we asked him, he'd brush it off, spinning stories that didn't quite add up. It wasn't until much later that we learned the truth. He was lying to protect her, covering up her violence, even as he was being torn down in ways we could hardly imagine.

Beyond Physical Violence

Domestic violence isn't just physical. Yes, physical abuse is brutal, and the scars it leaves are visible, but the wounds from emotional and mental abuse cut the deepest. They are the wounds that tear someone down from the inside out, slowly, piece by piece, until the person they once were becomes unrecognizable. And that's what happened to my brother. He wasn't just a victim of physical aggression; he was a victim of words that cut deeper than any knife, of manipulation that twisted his perception of himself, of emotional games that left him second-guessing his worth.

Breaking Stereotypes: Men as Victims

People often think of domestic violence as a one-sided story-the man being the aggressor, and the woman the victim. But that's not always the case. There are plenty of women who use manipulation and emotional abuse to dominate, to control, to push a man to his breaking point. They know exactly how to undermine his confidence, how to provoke him, how to chip away at his sense of self until he doesn't even recognize his own reflection. And when he reacts, when he finally snaps, it's his actions that get judged; not hers. We see the aftermath, but we rarely see the buildup-the constant taunting, the psychological warfare, the deliberate prodding until he can't take it anymore.

Let me be clear: I am not excusing or justifying violence in any form. A man should never lay a hand on a woman, no matter what she says or does. But I also believe that we have to acknowledge the role some women play in these toxic dynamics. There are women who are domestically violent, and there are men who suffer in silence because society tells them they are supposed to be strong, hold it all together, and never show weakness. Men are expected to endure, to brush off the insults, to withstand the emotional blows without flinching. And when they do finally break, it's often too late-they've already internalized the damage.

The Silent Struggle

Men don't often talk about the emotional and mental abuse they face. They don't tell anyone when their partner is tearing them down from the inside, when the words she speaks are making them feel small, worthless, and incapable. They don't share the stories of how their spirit is crushed by constant belittlement, how their motivation and sense of purpose slowly slip away. They suffer in silence, trying to hold on to their dignity while being torn apart by someone who is supposed to love them. And if there's unhealed trauma lingering beneath the surface, those words-those emotional cuts-can reopen wounds that were never truly healed. Toxic relationships don't just hurt the present; they unmask the past and reveal old scars. For men who have been taught to be strong and never show vulnerability, admitting they are in a damaging relationship is almost impossible. They stay silent, hoping it will get better, hoping they can fix it, hoping that if they just try harder, love a little more, or change a little more, it will all work out.

But it rarely does. Toxic relationships have a way of diminishing a person's character, breaking down their self-worth, and sapping their confidence. They drain the motivation to keep fighting, to keep pushing, to keep moving forward. You watch someone you love become a shadow of who they once were, and it's heartbreaking. You see the toll it takes on their mental and emotional well-being, the way their personality shifts, the way they start to believe the lies they've been told. It's like watching someone drown while you're standing helplessly on the shore, unable to reach them. We need to talk about this. We need to acknowledge the reality that men can be victims of domestic violence, too-victims of emotional and mental abuse that can leave scars far deeper than any bruise or broken bone. We have to create a safe space for them to speak, to share, to be vulnerable without judgment. We have to tell our men that it's okay to feel, to hurt, to seek help. They don't have to be tough all the time; they don't have to hold it all in.

Men need a voice, they need a place to heal, and they need to know that they are not alone. Domestic violence affects everyone-men and women alike-and until we acknowledge that, until we stop seeing it as a one-sided issue, we'll never truly be able to bring healing to those who are suffering in silence.

Unbroken Key Takeaways

- Domestic violence is not just physical; emotional and mental abuse are often present.

- The scars of emotional abuse can be deeper and more lasting than physical ones. Emotional manipulation, belittlement, and taunting can slowly strip away a person's confidence and sense of self-worth.

- Domestic violence is often portrayed as a one-sided issue, with men depicted as the aggressors. However, women can also be perpetrators, using emotional and psychological abuse to control their partners.

- Men who are victims of emotional and mental abuse often don't speak out, fearing judgment or not wanting to appear vulnerable. This silence prevents healing and contributes to the deepening of emotional wounds.

Unbroken Reflection Questions

1. Have you ever witnessed someone you care about fall into a toxic relationship? What signs did you see that might have indicated the presence of emotional or mental abuse?

2. How do you think emotional abuse impacts a person's overall well-being, compared to physical abuse? Why is it important to address both?

3. What can we do as a community to raise awareness about domestic violence being a problem for both men and women, and encourage healing and support for victims of all genders?

CHAPTER NINE

Forgiveness

"Then Peter came to him and asked, 'Lord, how often should I forgive someone who sins against me? Seven times?' 'No, not seven times,' Jesus replied, 'but seventy times seven!'"

Matthew 18:21-22 (NLT)

The Initial Choice to Forgive

"What do you mean forgive? Why forgive someone who hurt you? Someone who took something away from you. Someone who had a choice to make another decision but decided to do a malicious act anyway. She doesn't deserve my forgiveness." These statements were just some of what the people around me were saying, and sometimes they were my own thoughts when my mind would run wild. Most wouldn't believe it but within minutes of hearing words I never wanted or thought I would hear, "We did all we could do", I opened my mouth in my moment of crying out to God and said, "I forgive her". I know most are saying "WHAT?" as you read the last statement. It's a very common phrase I hear when sharing my story. Yea I forgive her. Now don't get me wrong, I was mad; I was extremely mad but it's not my job to punish her. Nothing I could say or do to her would bring my brother back or make it feel better. Nothing at all.

I realized a couple of things-she was hurting, there were people in her life that either didn't show up from her to get the right help or give her the guidance she needed to regulate her emotions and negative thoughts, and she was not given the proper coping skills. I mean preceding this as you have read, she was manipulative, and verbally and physically abusive. She needed help to change her negative emotions and character traits. She needed support in processing and healing from past traumas unrelated to my brother. So, if I was not going to forgive her, I would have to also include a long list of others who didn't show up for her. Just think what if she had received the proper support, guidance and healing she required, I wouldn't be writing this book. But who am I to judge or condemn?

I've never literally murdered someone, but we all have caused pain to someone emotionally and mentally by our actions or words. If I was going to place her in the hot seat, I would need to sit right next to her for my sins-no matter how small I may feel they were compared to what she did. Now I'm not trying to say that she wasn't surrounded by family or people who love her. Maybe they didn't have the tools to help her or to guide her in the right direction to get the help she needed, or maybe they got her help, and the help wasn't what she needed. I just felt like if I'm going to be mad at her, then I need to be mad at everyone. I truly believe that everyone plays a part. It's not like one person alone causes something to happen. The way someone is brought up, the trauma they face, the environments they live in, etc., all play a part in who they are and what they do.

Breaking the Cycle of Trauma

Do you know if my brother was whole, if he truly loved himself, if he was completely healed himself then it would've been easier for him to walk away. He would've been wise enough to walk away and not continue to stay in a toxic situation. When we have unhealed trauma then we develop a trauma bound with others thinking it's real love. Sometimes, if we continue to carry people, they basically make us their God instead of calling on God. It's almost like enabling them, but once you remove yourself from the picture, then they have no choice but to either find another person, go to God, and/or go to therapy and truly get the help that they need to get better. Something that some people don't realize about forgiveness is forgiveness is not about the other person. I know one thing for sure, I don't want to miss out on my blessings and experience all that God has for me because I refuse to forgive. And I know for sure God can do more than I could ever do. He would not just let this go without punishment. At the end of the day when I face God on judgment day, He wouldn't care about me saying, "Well God she did this, so I did this to hurt her and to get revenge." He is going to say, "I don't care what she did, you are held accountable for your actions. Her actions do not excuse your decisions." Being able to forgive her and give it all to God, helps me open my eyes to God and His plan. I could never forget what she did, but I could trust God to make all things work for my good. I could trust God to turn my pain into joy.

The Cost of Unforgiveness

People think saying things or doing things to the person that caused their pain is going to make them feel better. But it doesn't at all, because after you do or say what you feel, guess what, you still feel the hurt. Nothing changed. The pain still stings. Holding onto a grudge and unwillingness to forgive will only hurt you even more. All we do when we hold on is harden our hearts, not just to the person that hurts us but those around us. We became bitter, resentful, frustrated, angry and we held on to countless negative emotions without a reason. We become blind to the truth before us and can't see anyone/anything for what it is because we can now only see from hurt eyes. Forgiving those who have hurt us will allow us to keep our power and walk in healing.

We cannot fully heal from hurt and pain unless we forgive others and ourselves.

My Journey with Forgiveness

This was not my first rodeo of forgiving someone who had hurt me, and I'm sure it's not my last. Forgiveness for the most part has always come easy to me. I've never been a person to hold grudges or hold on to things. Maybe it was the people pleaser in me, but I could never stay mad at people who hurt me for long. I was always quick to forgive. I have always been the type of person to see both sides of the story and understand both perspectives. Please understand that even though I was able to forgive people, it doesn't mean that I still didn't hurt. It doesn't mean that I forgot what they have done to me. Forgiveness is about you. When you hold on to what someone has done to hurt you, that person has power over you. You are triggered and angered by that person. You spend a lot of time and energy thinking about the person. But when you allow yourself to let go, you allow God to do what only God can do, and you free yourself from the bondage of unforgiveness. When you are unforgiving, it can completely blind you, you cannot see clearly nor fully understand their perspective because you are seeing people from unforgiving eyes. It's important for us to see people the way that God sees them, not based on our past trauma or hurt. I knew that my brother's girlfriend had some things going on and I also knew that there was good in her; but she was never put in the right place to get the help that she needs to allow her light to shine brighter than the bad.

The Process of Letting Go

Forgiveness is a journey. I was able to forgive that same night, whereas for other people, it may take days, weeks, or even years.

However long it might take you, just start the journey. Pray and ask God to open your eyes, to heal your heart, to help you let go of the person who has hurt you or caused you pain. There's a chance you may never hear "I'm sorry" or get an explanation and you have to learn to be okay with it. You must trust in God's word to say he will make all things work for our good. All things, not some things. He is close to the brokenhearted, and those who are crushed in spirit. His word says that He will turn in the morning. It's a joyous praise. He says he will turn out despair. You have to trust that even during that painful journey that God has a plan and a purpose. And another thing-who are we to draw judgment? Are we perfect people?

Who are we to judge someone else? Yes, we may have not done the same thing that they have done, but we are yet sinners, and when Jesus died on the cross, he did not say that I'm only forgiving the people who've done this or that, he said he has forgiven all of us. The word of God also says that he will not forgive us, unless we forgive those who have sinned against us. So, in order for God to forgive us, we have to forgive others, and this is another reason why I choose to not hold onto hurt caused by other people. I choose to let go and let God do what only he can do. I have an understanding that some people were not given the tools they need in life, and they're only acting out of the way that they were raised. We can't expect people to talk, walk, act and respond like we would. With the proper tools and fully trusting God, what seems difficult and impossible is made easy.

I challenge you to let go of the person(s) who hurt you. Keep in mind that just because you forgive someone it doesn't mean that they have to continue to be in your life-you can let them go. Don't wait for your apology. Don't wait for the explanation; just know and stand on God's truth and God's word. If you're struggling with forgiveness, talk to God about it and ask him to give you the tools and strategies to let go. Keep in mind that it is a process, and you have to give yourself grace. One minute you may be fine, but the next day you might find yourself angry again. But just give it to God.

FORGIVENESS PRAYER AND CONFESSION

Lord, I come to you to ask for your help in forgiving **<Name>** for **<what they did to you>**. Lord, I am struggling to forgive **<Name>** for what they did to me because it really hurt me deeply. Lord as I release them to you, please let me completely let it go. I trust that you will heal my heart and help me move past this hurt. Lord, I did not want to hold any unforgiveness in my heart. I really need your help to release them. Please give me wisdom and understanding on how to move forward, Lord. Lord hear my cry, heal my heart. In the name of Jesus. Amen.

Unbroken Key Takeaways

- Forgiveness is not about the other person; it's about your freedom. Holding on to unforgiveness will only hurt you more and keep you in bondage.

- Forgiveness can feel impossible, especially when someone has hurt you deeply. But forgiveness is a choice, and it doesn't mean you forget the pain or that you justify their actions.

- Unhealed trauma often leads to destructive patterns. When you forgive, you stop the cycle and give God the opportunity to heal both you and the other person.

- Forgiveness is not a one-time event, but a continuous process. It may take time, and that's okay. Be patient with yourself and trust God to heal your heart.

- Only God can judge. When you hold on to anger and refuse to forgive, you take on the role of judgment, which isn't your responsibility.

- Extend grace to yourself in the process of forgiveness.

Unbroken Reflection Questions

1. Have you been holding onto unforgiveness in any area of your life? How has it affected your peace and emotional well-being?

2. Can you recall a time when forgiveness was difficult, but you chose to forgive? How did it feel once you made that choice?

3. In what ways can you begin the process of forgiveness, even if it takes time? What steps can you take today?

4. How can you remind yourself that forgiveness is for your healing and freedom, not just for the person who hurt you?

5. Do you find it difficult to let go of judgment and trust God's justice? What does it look like for you to let God handle the situation?

6. How can you extend grace to yourself while going through the journey of forgiveness?

CHAPTER TEN

The World That Always Fails

"Dear friends, never take revenge. Leave that to the righteous anger of God. For the Scriptures say, I will take revenge; I will pay them back,' says the Lord."

Romans 12:19 (NLT)

"Wow really you must be kidding me. How could you let her go with just time served, community services, low court fees and a F on her record. She took a whole life. She took a son. She took a brother. She took a young black male who meant the world to many. FREE? She's Free?! What kind of Justice is this? I bet if it was my brother on trial he would be in jail." These were just some of the many thoughts that ran through my mind the day we had court regarding my brother's murder and the days preceding her release. I was in shock. I was in disbelief. So many emotions and at this point most weren't good. I could not understand how they could just let her go FREE. She served less than 2 years for taking someone's life. This day was supposed to be a day of celebration, not just because of the trial date but because it was my daughter's high school graduation.

We were at the graduation on Zoom for the trial since they were still having virtual court sessions. It was so hard for me to be present at my daughter's graduation, thinking about everything that was happening on the zoom. I had to also speak on behalf of my family and what this situation has done to us. We were not happy at all about the outcome and just kept thinking what we could do or what we could have done differently. It felt like they didn't care about my brother's life or take into consideration that she had other choices she could have made. But the fact that she had a recording on her phone of my brother apologizing for putting his hands on her led to the judge (a black female judge) to rule in her favor. Let's remember that they both put hands on each other often, this was not a one-sided abusive relationship.

Even with all of the negative emotions, I continue to claim victory. I kept saying it may seem like we have lost but victory is ours. Someone being free from a physical prison does not mean they are mentally and emotionally free. Her freedom comes with a cost, and she will never forget what she did.

I could not stop asking, "Lord what are you up to? Please help me understand. First my brother's life is taken and now he doesn't receive any justice. Lord, I trusted you to serve justice. I prayed, my family prayed, friends prayed, and even complete strangers prayed. I just knew deep in my heart you would give us justice. Lord, how does my brother get the justice he deserves? His life meant something; his absence has caused so much pain to so many. Lord, help me use your hands."

Like come on, she had a choice at that moment. She could have walked away but no; she continued to engage in an agreement and then proceeded to take a life. No one was holding her down. No one was stopping her from leaving. No one was threatening her. She was the threat. She was the one who wouldn't walk away or leave it alone. She was the one who decided to go into my parents' kitchen to get a knife and stab my brother. Not just one time but several. And it's almost like she knew exactly where to stab him to cause the most harm. She was supposed to love him. Why wasn't she emotionally mature enough just to walk away and leave it alone. How could the judge not give justice when justice was due. How could she let someone go free for taking another person's life when the person had other options. I mean less than 2 years and she is set free. What kind of corrupt system is this?

For the next couple of days, I just rested in God's presence. I didn't talk to anyone, I barely responded to texts. Only communicated to those in my house and closest to me. I had to process what just happened. I couldn't process what the world had to offer; I needed to process fully with God. I didn't need to hear other people's thoughts and opinions; I just needed to hear from God. In those moments with God, I was constantly reminded of His goodness, faithfulness, and unfailing love. I was reminded he will never leave nor forsake me. He cares about the things that burden me. He has given me a garment of praise for a spirit of heaviness. He reminded me that there is purpose in my pain, but I had to fully give him all of my pain without holding anything back.

That my brother was his child, and he cared about him more than I ever could. He wrapped me in his arms and told me he got it. Trust and believe me, justice will be served. He opened my eyes to see from a heavenly perspective and not a worldly perspective. He reminded me that he is still in control, and I had nothing to worry about. I had to focus on the tasks ahead and allow him to use me for his glory. God is our creator and sometimes we cannot see or understand his moves, but he is faithful and righteous in everything he does. I thank and praise God every day that we have not run into her, and I trust Him to continue to protect us from what could be a triggering moment.

Now let's talk about this corrupt system of ours-the system that failed my brother. The system where justice is barely served for black and brown people, especially our men. The system that allows offenders back on the street to continue to hurt others and families. Let's get into the facts and statistics:

According to the Coalition to End Domestic Violence website, each year 10,000 black men are unjustly handed a criminal record and labeled as "Abusers", even though black men usually are the victims of partner abuse. It was also noted that each year, 1.47 million Black men, compared to 1.38 million Black women, are victims of sexual violence, domestic violence, or stalking according to Centers for Disease Control, National Intimate Partner and Sexual Violence Survey: 2010-2012.

Domestic violence against Black men, in particular, is an issue often overlooked, yet it is a significant concern. Research from the National Intimate Partner and Sexual Violence Survey (NISVS), conducted by the CDC, indicates that about 40% of Black men experience intimate partner violence (domestic violence) in their lifetimes, which includes physical violence, psychological aggression, and stalking by a partner. Although this figure includes a wide range of abuses, it highlights that Black men are indeed affected by domestic violence on a substantial scale. Around 14.7% of Black men experience severe physical violence from an intimate partner during their lifetime, including being hit with a fist or something hard, beaten, slammed against something, or choked[4].

Let's be clear-these reported numbers may be higher than reported. Studies show that men, in general, are less likely to report instances of domestic violence due to stigma, societal expectations, and fear of not being believed. For Black men, this hesitancy is often compounded by concerns related to racial discrimination within the justice system, fear of appearing "weak," and distrust of law enforcement. Black men who experience domestic violence often have fewer support services available or feel unwelcome in existing support systems that focus on women, increasing their vulnerability to violence and reducing the likelihood of them seeking help. Additionally, stereotypes of Black men as aggressors can make it difficult for them to be seen as victims.

This bias can lead to situations where Black male victims are treated as perpetrators, especially if police are called in cases where both partners are Black. This concern often discourages Black men from reporting abuse, fearing that they will not be treated fairly. Research indicates that Black men who report domestic violence are more likely to face challenges in the legal system, including being wrongfully accused or having their cases dismissed due to bias. Also, let's not forget the judgment that they may feel will come from their family or friends as being weak or soft.

The experience of domestic violence can lead to severe psychological consequences for Black men, including increased rates of depression, anxiety, PTSD, and substance abuse as coping mechanisms. According to a report by the Substance Abuse and Mental Health Services Administration (SAMHSA), Black men exposed to trauma, including domestic violence, are at higher risk of mental health issues and face barriers in accessing culturally competent mental health care. Let me ask you a question, how would you feel if you didn't have a person you could trust or a safe place to turn in your time of need? What if you couldn't trust the people who are put in the positions to help you? Our black men are placed in a position to just deal with it, to just figure it out or, sadly, just take matters into our hands. We are leaving our black men with feelings of hopelessness and despair-let's not forget with unhealed trauma. Because of the isolation, trauma, and stigma associated with domestic violence amongst all men, including Black men, studies show they have a higher risk of suicide.

Black men are at a higher risk of experiencing severe outcomes in cases of domestic violence, including homicide. According to the Violence Policy Center, Black men are disproportionately represented in domestic violence homicide statistics. This emphasizes the importance of addressing and providing resources for Black men in abusive relationships. These statistics show that Black men are deeply affected by domestic violence and face unique barriers in seeking help and support. The intersection of race, gender stereotypes, and stigma creates a challenging environment for Black men experiencing domestic violence.

Unbroken Key Takeaways

- The legal system often fails, but true justice, even in the absence of a court ruling, is ultimately in God's hands.

- Faith in God's promises provides the strength to endure and overcome, even in the most painful situations.

Unbroken Reflection Questions

1. How does your faith help you cope with moments when justice seems delayed or denied? What role does forgiveness play in healing during difficult times?

2. How can you advocate for those who may not have the resources or support to speak out about their pain, especially for marginalized groups such as Black men?

3. Reflecting on the pain of losing a loved one, how do you find healing in moments of grief? What practices or faith-based principles bring you comfort?

4. How do you navigate feelings of hopelessness and despair in your own life, and how can you support others who may be experiencing similar emotions?

CHAPTER ELEVEN

The One Who Never Fails

"It is the same with my word. I send it out, and it always produces fruit. It will accomplish all I want it to, and it will prosper everywhere I send it."

Isaiah 55:11 (NLT)

Love's First Teacher

My brother was the very first man who showed me what it truly means to be seen, loved, and appreciated. He was the one who helped me realize my worth when I couldn't see it myself. For most of my life, I struggled with self-love. I struggled with the idea that I was worthy of love or that I even deserved it. Growing up as a fatherless child left a gaping hole in my heart. I never heard my father's voice tell me I was beautiful, or that he loved me, or that I mattered. There was always an emptiness in me-an echo where those words should have been. But Dante, my brother, filled that void with his love, a love that was never hesitant or conditional.

Dante made sure I knew how he felt about me, not just with his words, but through his actions. He didn't just say "I love you," he showed me every single day. He had this way of speaking directly to my soul. It was as if he could read my heart; like he knew the words that had been missing all my life. He would look at me and tell me how proud he was of me, how much he believed in me, and how-in his eyes-I was perfect just as I was. He made me feel like I could do anything. It was as if he could see the parts of me that I couldn't see in myself yet. He was my mirror, reflecting back the beauty and strength I had buried deep inside.

God's Love Through Dante

Now, as I sit here reflecting on those moments, I realize it wasn't just Dante's love-it was God's love shining through him. God used my brother as His vessel, showing me what unconditional, unbreakable love looks like. Through Dante, I experienced a glimpse of God's heart: a heart that doesn't judge, doesn't condemn, and doesn't keep score. Dante's love was forgiving, no matter what I did or said. He never held a grudge, and he never stopped loving me. That's what true love is. That's God's love-a love that sees beyond flaws, that loves us in our mess, and that picks us up when we fall. My brother's love for me was a glimpse into God's true nature-a nature so much more profound and deeper than I could have ever imagined. In Dante's presence, I saw the traits of God that I had only read about come to life. God's faithfulness, His holiness, His compassion, His righteousness, and His boundless love became more than just words on a page—they became the very air I breathed, the truth I clung to, and the foundation that sustained me.

The Character of God

Understanding God's character was the only thing that helped me stand again after losing my brother. There were days when the weight of grief pressed so heavily on my chest that I could hardly breathe. Days when it felt like the world was dark, and nothing made sense. But I knew there was only one place I could turn for comfort. I leaned deeply into God's word and clung to His promises like they were my lifeline. Because, honestly, nothing in this world could help me make sense of losing Dante. No words, no actions, and no empty condolences could reach that broken part of my heart. But God's word did. His words poured into the cracks, slowly filling the emptiness with His presence, comfort, and strength.

God is faithful. He does not turn away when life gets hard. When I lost Dante, I felt shattered, like my entire world had crumbled to dust. Yet in the darkest nights of my grief, God remained. He didn't leave when my anger boiled over or when I screamed in silence, questioning why this happened. He stayed. He held me. He listened to every cry and every question without judgment, and when I was ready, He spoke gently to my heart. His faithfulness is not dependent on my perfection or my ability to handle everything. He is faithful simply because that's who He is. No matter how deep the pain, God was there, and He never wavered.

Even in my anger, even in my sorrow, He was unwaveringly present. His faithfulness isn't like that of a person, who might walk away or become impatient. No, God is the one who stays through the long, exhausting nights and the empty, aching days. He promises to never leave us or forsake us, and I found that to be true in the most tangible way. He was the friend who never walked away, the comforter who never stopped comforting, and the anchor that held me steady when everything else seemed to be falling apart. His promises became the truth I needed to hear, a solid rock I could stand on when the ground felt like it was crumbling beneath my feet.

God is holy. I learned that His holiness doesn't mean He is distant or untouchable. It means that He is pure, without blemish, and completely separate from the brokenness of this world. In His holiness, God has a perspective that I could never understand. He sees the end from the beginning, and while I couldn't make sense of losing my brother, I knew that God's plan was bigger than my pain. I realized that

His holiness means His ways are higher, His thoughts are greater, and He is in control even when everything feels out of control. His holiness is the reason I could trust Him when I couldn't trust myself to make sense of the chaos. It's because of His holiness that I found a sense of peace, knowing that He is sovereign, perfect, and infinitely good-even when life doesn't feel good.

And yet, this holy God is also loving. It's hard to understand that a God so majestic, so pure, and so powerful could also be so deeply personal. Yet, He is. In His love, He didn't just watch me from a distance while I suffered-He stepped into my pain and carried it with me. His love is not conditional or earned. I didn't have to do anything to make God love me; He already did, just as I was, broken and hurting. His love was patient when I was impatient, forgiving when I was filled with bitterness, and tender when my heart was hard. Even when I didn't have the words to pray, God's love wrapped around me, filling the empty spaces, speaking to the places of my heart that words couldn't reach.

God is compassionate. When I was at my lowest, He didn't come to me with condemnation or judgment. He came with compassion. God saw every tear I cried, and He didn't rush me to "get over it" or to move past the pain. He wept with me. I felt His presence so close, like He was sitting beside me, holding me as I cried. He reminded me that He is a God who knows sorrow, who understands grief, and who is familiar with our suffering. Jesus Himself experienced heartbreak, betrayal, and loss, and in that way, God wasn't a distant deity who couldn't relate to my struggles. He was right there, understanding my pain on the most intimate level. His compassion gave me permission to grieve, to feel, to be vulnerable without fear of rejection.

And then, there's His righteousness. In the face of injustice, God is a righteous judge. He sees all, knows all, and is committed to truth and justice. Losing my brother the way I did brought up so many questions about justice and fairness. I wrestled with anger and frustration, feeling as if the world had wronged me in the most grievous way. Yet, God reminded me that His righteousness is not like the world's. He sees beyond the surface, into the deepest motivations of the heart, and He will bring about true justice in His time. I had to learn to let go of my need to seek vengeance and to trust in His righteous nature. I learned that God's justice is perfect and that He can handle what I cannot. Trusting in His righteousness allowed me to release the weight of bitterness and to move forward in forgiveness.

Every time I opened my Bible, I saw these characteristics of God woven into the stories of those who had come before me-those who had faced heartache, loss, betrayal, and suffering, just as I had. And every time, God proved Himself to be faithful, loving, compassionate, righteous, and holy. He was with Moses in the desert, comforting Hannah in her barrenness, walking with David through his darkest valleys, and bringing new life to the broken heart of Mary Magdalene. This is the same God who was with me when I felt utterly alone, the same God who picked up the shattered pieces of my heart and began to make me whole again.

There's something else about God's character that I cannot overlook-He is a Redeemer. He doesn't just bring comfort; He takes the ashes of our brokenness and turns them into something beautiful. He is in the business of redeeming what was lost and restoring what was stolen. Even in my grief, even in the injustice of it all, I began to see that God was still at work. He was redeeming my pain, using it to bring healing to others, and turning my mourning into a message of hope. That's what a Redeemer does. He doesn't waste our pain but repurposes it for a greater good.

I want you to know that God is not only capable of carrying you through your pain; He is eager to do so. He is not only able to bring you peace; He wants to fill you with a peace that surpasses all understanding. This is the God who numbers every hair on your head, who knows every thought before you speak it, and who has engraved your name on the palms of His hands. His character is not something to be studied from a distance-it's something to be experienced, lived, and felt deep in your soul.

You're loved by God who is perfectly faithful, infinitely compassionate, and utterly holy. You are seen by a God who is righteous and just, who will not let evil have the final word. You are held by a God who knows your name, who knows your pain, and who promises that He will walk with you every step of the way. He is everything you need—your comforter, your healer, your shield, your strength, and your friend. He is enough, even when everything else falls apart. That's what kept me going; knowing that the God who walked with me through my darkest valley was the same God who would lead me to brighter days. I learned that my grief did not define me, my pain did not limit me, and my loss did not have the final word—because God's love and His promises always have the final say.

Scripture after scripture, I was reminded of His faithfulness. I read over and over that He was with me, even in my darkest valley, that He would never leave me or forsake me. That He cared for me, and that I could lay my heavy burdens at His feet. I read about mourning being turned into joy, about beauty rising from ashes, and about a peace that surpasses all understanding. God became the anchor that held me steady when the waves of grief threatened to drown me.

The world took Dante from me, and I won't lie-there were moments when bitterness and rage bubbled inside of me, threatening to consume me. How could the person who stole my brother's life walk free, untouched by the pain she caused? But then I heard God's whisper, asking me to forgive, to rise above, and to be a light in this darkness. I had to make a choice-to allow the darkness of grief and unforgiveness to steal the light within me, or to reclaim my power and choose healing. I chose the latter. I had to; because I knew there were others, like me, who were drowning in pain and needed to see that healing was possible.

I decided to step out of my comfort zone and help others heal. To show them that there is life after loss, and hope after heartbreak. I wanted people to know that even in their deepest pain, God's love is there, waiting to wrap them up and lead them out of the darkness. There are so many who don't realize they are in toxic relationships, who don't know they deserve better, who need to be shown what healthy love looks like. There are families struggling to find meaning in their grief, parents trying to understand how to keep living when a piece of their heart is gone, and individuals who believe they'll never smile or laugh again. But I know-because I've lived it-that God can turn even the deepest pain into joy. I know that Dante's life, though cut short, still has a mighty purpose. His story, and my journey of healing, will be a beacon for others.

I don't know what loss or pain you may be facing. I don't know what you've had to let go of or what has been ripped away from you. But I do know this-you are not alone. You have the power to rise from the ashes and declare that pain does not get the final word. You have a choice in who gets to write the final chapter of your story. You have a God who loves you fiercely, who fights for you, who sees you exactly as you are, and who will never abandon you. He is waiting, with open arms, to embrace your brokenness, to wipe your tears, and to fill you with a peace that no one can take away. You have a future, a purpose, and a destiny that no loss can steal. Take this declaration to heart, and let it become a part of your daily walk:

A Declaration of Faith

I will no longer allow grief, loss, or the pain of this world to steal the best parts of me.

I am powerful.

I am victorious.

I am loved.

I am a child of the Most High.

I will not be afraid, because He is my Helper, and He will never leave or forsake me.

I am exactly who He says I am.

Watch out world—I'm back, and I see clearly now.

An Invitation to Healing

Write it down. Speak it out loud. Let it echo in your heart and soul until it drowns out every lie and every fear. Are you ready to let the best parts of you-the parts that God Himself planted inside of you-change the world? What territory in your heart have you given to the enemy? It's time to take it back!

I know you might be weary. I know you might feel like you have no strength left. But I'm here to tell you that you do. You have a fight left in you; a fire that hasn't been extinguished. You have a Father who knows your pain, who holds every broken piece of your heart in His hands, and who is ready to move on your behalf. This is the God who promises to give you beauty for ashes, joy for mourning, and peace that the world cannot comprehend. He can make you whole again. He can bring life back to your weary soul. I know, because He did it for me. So, I ask you-are you ready to try Him? What have you got to lose?

Unbroken Key Takeaways

- Even in moments of deep pain and grief, God remains faithful. His promises are true, and His presence is unshakeable, offering comfort and strength when nothing else can.

- God's character is one of holiness, compassion, righteousness, and justice. God does not abandon us in our suffering but steps into it with us, offering comfort, love, and compassion.

- God's character as a Redeemer is essential. He doesn't waste our pain but uses it for His greater purpose. Even in loss, God redeems our brokenness and turns it into something beautiful.

- In the face of loss and grief, choose healing over bitterness. The decision to forgive and rise above pain allows you to experience God's love and extend that healing to others.

Unbroken Reflection Questions:

1. Can you think of a time when you experienced unconditional love? How did that love impact your sense of worth and identity?

2. When facing difficult situations or grief, how do you remind yourself of God's faithfulness? What promises in Scripture do you cling to in those moments?

3. What aspects of God's character stand out most to you—His holiness, His compassion, His righteousness, or His faithfulness? How have you experienced these characteristics in your own life?

4. Reflect on a painful or challenging time in your life. How can you see God's redeeming power at work in that situation now?

CHAPTER TWELVE

Honoring

"So you have sorrow now, but I will see you again; then you will rejoice, and no one can rob you of that joy."

John 16:22 (NLT)

Dante was 3 months and 3 days from his 23rd birthday. November 15, 2020, was supposed to be just another day we gathered together to celebrate another year of Dante's life; a day filled with joy, laughter, and the warmth of family and friends surrounding him. Instead, it became the first of many celebrations without him physically present. Even writing those words makes my heart ache all over again. My God, it hurts so much to know that those moments are memories now and not plans for the future.

Yet, despite the pain, I knew we had to find a way to honor him. Dante's life was about so much more than the way it ended. It was about the way he lived, how he showed up, the way he cared for others, and the genuine kindness he spread. I couldn't just let his birthday pass without honoring that light. So, we decided to give back in the best way we knew how. We organized a community giveback in our childhood neighborhood, giving out coats, food, and other necessities. It was exactly the type of thing Dante would have loved. He had such a big heart, and he thrived on taking care of others. I could practically feel his presence that day, as if he was walking around with us, smiling, talking to everyone, and spreading that joy he was well known for, and ultimately proud that we were choosing to honor him in such a meaningful way. It was such a good day. A day where grief and celebration coexisted, where sorrow was tempered by the act of giving, and where his memory was alive in every kind gesture we extended to others. Each coat handed out, each meal given, each face that lit up with gratitude was a tribute to who Dante was at his core.

Now, every year, we make a point to celebrate his birthday and the anniversary of his passing. Sometimes, it's another giveback in his honor, pouring love back into the community that shaped us both. Other times, it's a vacation to a place he would have loved, a visit to one of his favorite restaurants, or a big celebration where family and friends gather to share stories, laughter, and the love that still binds us. These moments are our way of keeping his spirit alive, of letting the world know that Dante mattered, that he was loved, and that his legacy of generosity and care continues.

The first year after losing him-the year of "firsts"-was one of the hardest seasons I have ever walked through. Every holiday, every milestone, every ordinary day without him was a reminder of his absence. After his birthday, we went straight into the holiday season-Thanksgiving and Christmas; holidays that should have been spent with Dante's bright smile lighting up the room. For Thanksgiving, we made sure to cook his favorite dishes, keeping him close to our hearts through the tastes and smells he loved so much. We'd sit around the table, sharing stories about him, laughing, and, yes, crying too. It wasn't the same without him, but it was our way of bringing him into the moment and not allowing his memory to fade.

At Christmas, we placed three battery-operated candles next to his photo by the tree. Those flickering lights were our way of saying that his light still shines, even in the darkest moments. We decorated his grave, placing ornaments and lights around his resting place, as if to remind him, and ourselves, that he was still part of our Christmas celebration. Those small gestures were ways to honor him, to feel close to him, and to remind ourselves that he was still with us in spirit. Being surrounded by family and friends during the holidays was crucial. It created a safe space to grieve, to remember, and to heal together. We told stories, shared our favorite memories, and laughed at the moments that made Dante who he was-full of life, laughter, and love. There was something so healing about being honest with each other about our grief and still choosing to celebrate, to find joy amidst the pain.

Each and every day, we are committed to honoring Dante by how we live. It's not just about marking special occasions or visiting his resting place; it's about embodying the love he shared and letting that love shape our daily lives. It's in the little things like working hard, showing up for others, offering a kind word to a stranger, and being a light in a world that often feels so dark. We carry his legacy with us every single day, not just in big, grand gestures but in the ordinary ways we choose to be present, to love, and to care.

Carrying on His Legacy: Brothers with Tools

One of the most meaningful ways we plan to honor Dante is by carrying forward his vision and legacy, through his dream of making a difference for young Black men. Dante started a business called Brothers with Tools, a small but powerful initiative dedicated to providing skills, opportunities, and mentorship for young Black men. This business wasn't just about tools in the literal sense; it was about equipping young men with the tools they needed to succeed in life. Dante believed deeply in lifting others up, in helping them break free from cycles of struggle, and in showing that there is another way; a way that leads to dignity, opportunity, and success.

We have committed ourselves to restarting Brothers with Tools and turning it into a full-fledged nonprofit in his honor. This nonprofit will serve as a beacon of hope, creating a safe space for young Black males to thrive. Our goal is to provide mentoring, therapy, and personal development opportunities that Dante would have loved to offer himself. We want to be there for these young men, guiding them away from the statistics that too often define Black males in this country; statistics that paint them as part of a system that fails to see their potential, their talent, and their worth. Dante was determined to be more than a statistic. He was a shining example of what happens when someone is given a chance to succeed—when someone sees your worth, invests in your potential, and gives you the tools you need to build a better future. Through "Brothers with Tools", we are going to do just that-shine a more positive light on the young Black men we mentor, empowering them to rise above the expectations of a society that often underestimates them.

We will offer programs that focus on professional development, life skills, emotional well-being, and therapy because mental health is just as important as any other skill. We want to provide a sanctuary where young men can heal, grow, and learn without fear of judgment. We want to create an environment where they can be vulnerable, where they can express their struggles, and where they can find a brotherhood that encourages and uplifts them. This nonprofit is about more than carrying on Dante's legacy; it's about helping other young men avoid the pitfalls that too often lead to a life trapped in cycles of systemic injustice. It's about giving them a chance to be seen, to be heard, and to be valued for who they are.

Dante's vision was to see young Black men succeed, to see them make choices that would lead them toward a future full of promise, instead of feeling cornered by circumstances beyond their control. We want to ensure that his dream doesn't fade away, and that his legacy lives on through every young man who walks through our doors and finds a new path for his life. For every life that is touched, for every young man who is mentored, loved, and guided, we honor Dante. We honor the brother who refused to let the world define him and who saw greatness in everyone he encountered.

Honoring Our Loved Ones—Now and Always

One vital lesson I learned after losing my brother is the importance of honoring our loved ones while they are still alive, while they can still hear our words and feel the weight of our love. It's easy to wait, to assume there's always more time, that another chance will come. But the truth is, we don't know what tomorrow holds, and our time with those we love is never guaranteed. I want to encourage you to give your loved ones their flowers now, while they can still hold them in their hands. Tell them you love them. Tell them why they matter to you. Celebrate their strengths, laugh at the silly things, and share the memories that bring you joy. Don't wait for the "right" moment— create those moments now.

If Dante taught me anything, it's that life is too precious to keep our love unspoken or our gratitude unexpressed. He lived fully, he loved fiercely, and he gave freely. And I want to live like that, too. I want to make sure the people I care about know it; not when they are gone, but while they are still here. I don't want to have regrets about words left unsaid or love left unexpressed.

I challenge you! Don't wait until it's too late to honor the people who mean the most to you. Don't wait for a tragedy to bring you together or for a loss to make you realize how much someone meant to you. Honor them now, in the everyday moments, in the conversations over coffee, in the unexpected phone calls, and in the simple gestures that show you care. We don't need to wait until someone is no longer with us to celebrate their life. We can do it now, while they can still see our smiles, hear our laughter, and feel our love. We can give them their flowers while they are still here to receive them, and in doing so, we not only honor them-we also honor the love and the light they bring into our lives. Dante's life reminds me every day to love deeply, to live fully, and to remind my loved ones that I care about them.

Meet Dante Eyasu

Dante Kidane Eyasu was a light in every room he walked into. That smile-the one that could brighten even the darkest of days-was contagious. He had this effortless way of making you feel seen and valued, whether you'd known him for a lifetime or were meeting him for the very first time. His presence was magnetic, a combination of warmth, humor, and undeniable charisma that just drew people in. When you were with Dante, you felt like you were with someone extraordinary; someone who carried a rare spirit of joy, kindness, and authenticity. Even after just a few moments in his company, you walked away with a piece of him imprinted on your heart.

Dante Kidane Eyasu gained his forever wings on August 12, 2020, and the world is a little dimmer without him. He was born on November 15, 1997, at Prince George's Hospital Center in Cheverly, Maryland, and was blessed with loving parents, Kidane Eyasu and Phyllis Foxx, who raised him to be the compassionate and hard-working young man he became. His sisters, Marcia Cole and Daniella Eyasu, were not just his siblings but his best friends, and he shared a special bond with his niece, Amaya, who was his partner-in-crime, and his nephews, Charles and Bryce, who adored their uncle. Dante was the kind of son, brother, uncle, and friend who would go to the ends of the earth for those he loved.

Dante graduated from Magruder High School in Rockville, Maryland, in 2016, a moment that marked the beginning of his journey as an ambitious young entrepreneur. With the help of his sisters, he launched Brothers with Tools, his first business venture-a project that was more than just a job to him; it was his passion. He took on moving and hauling jobs, junk removal, landscaping, and construction assistance throughout the Washington metropolitan area. His work ethic was unmatched, and his customers always praised him for being professional beyond his years. It wasn't just about the work itself for Dante; it was about serving people, and he poured his heart and soul into every job he took on. Dante had big dreams for Brothers with Tools, and there was no doubt he would have made those dreams a reality. He saw the potential for growth and was excited about where the future would lead.

But Dante wasn't just about business, he was about joy. He was the life of every party, and, just like his mom, he had a love for dancing that made him the heartbeat of every family gathering. Music was in his soul. He could spend hours DJing, playing old-school hits that had everyone jamming and singing along. It didn't matter if you were in a good mood or a bad one, when Dante was on the aux, you were going to have a good time. His energy was infectious, and he had this way of making everyone feel like they belonged, like they were part of something special.

Much like his dad, Dante had a knack for fixing things, especially when it came to technology. He was the go-to tech guy for friends and family, always ready to help troubleshoot a glitchy laptop or a slow Wi-Fi connection. He had that kind of patience and determination that made him excel at whatever he set his mind to. And beyond his tech skills, he had a passion for cars. You could often find him working under the hood, getting his hands dirty, and perfecting every detail of his beloved car. He was always excited to share the latest modifications he had made or to help a friend with car troubles, never expecting anything in return.

Dante loved deeply and lived fully. He was committed to his family, always talking about how he would take care of everyone one day. "Everything I do is for all of you," he would say, with a sincerity that was unmistakable. It wasn't just a promise; it was a declaration of how he lived his life-selflessly, and always putting others first.

Dante had a way of making you feel safe, like you could rely on him for anything, and he never hesitated to show up for the people he loved. Whether it was giving you the shirt off his back, offering a listening ear when you needed to talk, or showing up with a smile when you least expected it, Dante's giving spirit was unwavering. His famous words, "I got it, don't worry," will forever echo in the hearts of those who knew him. He meant it every single time, too. It didn't matter if he was exhausted, overwhelmed, or busy-if you needed something, he was there. Dante was a pillar of strength and reliability, not just for his family but for everyone he crossed paths with. There was maturity and wisdom in him far beyond his years, a kind of old soul insight that made him the person people turned to for advice, guidance, and comfort.

Dante had a way of making you feel like you were the most important person in the room. He was a listener, a thinker, and someone who genuinely cared. He made sure you knew that you mattered and that your problems were worth solving. He was often the person you went to when you needed a laugh, a boost of confidence, or a reminder that you could handle whatever life threw your way. He was always willing to offer wisdom, whether you were a kid or a grown adult—his insights were timeless, and he was wise far beyond his 22 years.

His absence has left an irreplaceable hole, not just in the lives of those who loved him, but in the world itself. Yet, his legacy of selflessness, generosity, and genuine love for others continues to live on through every memory shared, every laugh remembered, and every act of kindness performed in his honor.

Dante was a force-someone who wasn't just content with existing but lived life to its fullest, making a difference along the way. The memories, the laughter, the unforgettable moments will remain etched in the hearts of his family and friends forever.

The family invites everyone who knew Dante to keep his memory alive by embodying the values he held so dear- compassion, kindness, and love for one another. Let his spirit inspire you to reach out to others, to help without hesitation, and to love unconditionally. By living with the same grace and generosity that Dante showed in his too-short life, we keep his spirit with us. Dante Kidane Eyasu is forever in our hearts-a shining example of what it means to live with purpose, joy, and love. His laughter, his smile, his love, and his life are treasures that will never fade, no matter how much time passes.

Remembering Dante

As we close this chapter of Dante's life, we find ourselves reflecting on the impact he had on everyone who was fortunate enough to know him. While words can never fully capture the essence of who Dante was, they can help us remember and honor the spirit that he shared so generously with the world. He was a son, a brother, an uncle, a friend- roles he embraced with heart, dedication, and an undeniable light.

Dante left a legacy that cannot be measured by the years of his life but by the love, laughter, and lessons he shared along the way. His kindness, wisdom, and genuine joy were felt by everyone who crossed his path. Those who loved him most are now left with cherished memories, but even in his absence, his presence continues to resonate in the hearts of those he touched.

In this chapter, we invite you to read the reflections from those who knew Dante best. Through their words, you'll get a glimpse of the many ways he impacted lives, how he made each person feel seen and loved, and the profound ways in which he shaped the world around him. His legacy lives on in these stories, and through them, we keep his spirit alive. Dante may no longer be physically with us, but he will forever be a part of us, and these memories are a testament to the man he was and the love he continues to inspire.

Brother by Daniella Eyasu

Handsome, wise, and kind

There's no flaw I can find

The youngest child

And his siblings' best friend

I'll never understand why your life had to end

The world didn't deserve your beautiful spirit

Your voice, I can still here it

Your love, I can still feel it

Oh, my little brother, they'll never be another

You were more than

A businessman

A son

A brother

You were Gods artwork bought to life

I pray God heals our spirit and calms our heart

Overtime surroundings and people will change

I hope God's words never become strange

He will hear our cry's & feel our pain

With this loss we must kneel & pray

With God, great things we will gain

We love you today, yesterday, & tomorrow

Brother I won't complain

You'll be taken care of until we meet again

My uncle was such a light in my life. He was way more than an uncle; he was a brother to me. He always made sure I was ok. Anything I needed, Dante would provide, even if I never asked for it. It was never a dull moment with Dante. He always made everything fun and better. He was such a goofy person, always dancing, singing, and just goofing off. One thing about Dante was that he loved music. Anytime we get in the car he would always play his music and we would just jam singing our hearts out. But he was also such a selfless person, which I've always adored about him. He always would worry and provide for other people before himself. I'm so thankful for having him in my life.

- Amaya "My My"

Dante, my nephew, was all about family. He loved his family deeply. He had a heart for helping others and was always willing to do whatever he could to lend a hand. He looked out for everyone and made sure you felt cared for. Dante was a friendly, kind, and gentle man. I truly loved him, and so did everyone who had the privilege of knowing him. Nephew, you are truly missed.

- *Aunt Kim*

Dante…My little brother. My son. Where do I start. How do I put into words all the memories, all the laughs, the life lessons, car rides, family vacations, gaming sessions, meals and good times we shared. Dante we truly grew together. I grew as a man as you grew from a child to manhood. We sharpened each other. You show me unconditional love and admiration as an older brother / father figure, as I showed you the love of an older brother /father figure. This is going to be tough going back over the years. Let's start from the beginning.

I meet Dante in 2003 when he was about 6 years old. He was a super energetic kid with a magnetic personality. Marcia and I had been dating for some time when she invited me over to meet her family. Of course I was nervous to meet everyone. Dante instantly gravitated towards me and within minutes we were wrestling in the living room. Here I am trying to be polite and make a good impression when out of nowhere this kid jumps on me to test my strength. I remember him not giving me an inch of space that day. If we weren't wrestling, he was asking me 100 questions about everything he had no business asking about. Our relationship quickly progressed, and Dante would spend every weekend at our house. During the summer Dante and my little brother Alex were with us every year and every summer vacation. There was no seeing Paul and Marcia without Dante. Christmas, Thanksgiving, New Year, birthdays-whatever the occasion was-Dante was with us. We were inseparable. When Marcia and I were expecting our first son I remember sharing with her the weight I felt on my shoulders that I was now responsible for raising a man in this crazy world. She quickly assured me that this was nothing new for us, "look how great of a job you do with Dante and Alex". She was right, I had spent so much time with Dante over the years he was like a son to me. He truly helped me grow as a man. There were so many life lessons we shared that sharpened both of us. So much so that I was more than equipped for the task of raising a son. Dante was a person with strong character and an unbreakable sense of loyalty to his loved ones. Everything about Dante was focused around family and how he wanted to take care of us. He never spoke about himself; it was always about the family and his plan to provide a better life for everyone. He was a giving person; he was always more concerned about making sure everyone was good.

Dante was a man's man. He loved music, good food, combat sports and muscle cars. He also wore his heart on his sleeve and wasn't afraid to tell you he loved you. At the end of every conversation or if we were just casually saying goodbye Dante would make sure to let me know he loved me. We would talk for hours about so many different topics and his unique view on things. Because his heart was so pure, a lot of his views on things were from his loving heart. He saw the world and its people through his heart. He cared about people and wanted to help everyone he came in contact with. He had a heart for giving-one of the reasons he could never save money. He was quick to give it away. His philosophy was *"I'm blessed, other people need this money more than I do."*

Dante, thank you for being the man that you were. Thank you for being the brother that you were. Thank you for being the uncle that you were. Thank you for all the "I love you bro"; I'm blessed to have known you. I'm blessed to have been loved by you.

I love you Dante!

- *Paul*

Our son Dante was a cool child. He liked to work, configured and navigated on mobile phones/laptops and always volunteered to help others, regardless of how difficult the task may be. I'm going to miss his calls saying, "I'm just calling to check on you." Dante would tell me soon I'll be a businessman to take care of you, Mom and my sisters. As a parent I try to encourage him to take care of himself first and then to think about others. His death brings so much pain inflicted on me every passing day I have to think about him. Please keep us in your prayers. I and all my family thank you for attending his funeral, sending condolences and expressing your kind words.

- *Kidane (Dad)*

Dante where do I start. I love his smile no matter what was going on Dante would turn your frown into a smile once his presence was around you. Thoughtful of everyone no matter the situation and a caretaker of everyone he loved effortlessly.

- Dani F.

Dante, a young man who displayed love everywhere he went. A smile full of nothing but the love he brings to others. A SMILE full of LOVE for his beloved. Dante was the family's radiant sunshine.

- Aunt Linda

To the sweetest person I've ever known, you always kept me laughing with your goofy stories & unique personality. The amount of care and love you showed me since the first time I met you was like no other. You smiled even on your darkest days and you'd give your last if you had to without a doubt. Your heart & soul was so pure, an angel on earth and an even bigger angel in heaven. I thank God he allowed us to cross paths with each other, there's really nobody like you Dante. My heart breaks to see you go. You will always be in my heart. I love you forever, until we meet again my friend

- Diamond T.

Dante was a very kind and caring person. Who would help anybody that needs help? His legacy will always be remembered.

- Aunt Caroline

There is nothing more beautiful than a kind soul. Dante was full of love. No matter the time, he would always be there if u needed him. We are confident, yes, well pleased rather to be absent from the body and to be present with the Lord. You will forever hold a special place in my heart.

- Sharecka B.

Riverdale Tay was always just a call away and was guaranteed to brighten up your day. Dante always had a story to tell and when around Dante there was NEVER a dull moment. If you ever met Dante you would definitely never forget him or his positive energy. Dante will always be missed by many and NEVER forgotten I LOVE YOU LIL CUZ...watch over us until we meet again.

- Crystal Y.

Would do anything for anyone; big heart; treated everyone like family and with respect. He was always a phone call away and would give his last to make you happy. Beautiful smile; a young man who had big dreams that included everyone. Will be missed more than words can say. He deserves every feather in his wings to soar high in the sky.

- Lioma

Beautiful spirit and kind smile. Rambunctious and giving. Loving and kind. Always willing to lend a helpful hand. Take charge, the kind of leader who looked out for everyone in his circle. Boisterous personality, yet meek and respectful.

- Christine V.

Dante radiated positivity and love. Once he accepted people in his heart, he was fiercely loyal and always willing to lend a hand. He was deeply loved by his family and friends and will be terribly missed.

- Pauline C.

CONCLUSION

A Journey of Grief and Hope

As I bring this book to a close, I reflect on the journey we have taken together through these pages. Grief is a powerful and complex emotion that changes us forever. It challenges us, shapes us, and ultimately teaches us about the depth of our love and the strength we possess.

My brother, Dante, may no longer be here in physical form, but his spirit, his laughter, his kindness, and his dreams continue to live on in my heart and the hearts of all who knew and loved him. Through sharing my story, I hope to honor his memory and ensure that his legacy endures.

To those of you who are grieving, know that you are not alone. Your pain is valid, your journey is important, and your loved one's life matters. Allow yourself the space to grieve, to remember, and to heal. Surround yourself with supportive people who understand and respect your process. In moments of darkness, seek the light of faith, the comfort of friends and family, and the healing power of time. Remember that it's okay to smile again, to find joy, and to live fully. This does not diminish your love or the importance of the person you lost. Instead, it honors their memory by living a life that celebrates the time you had together. May you find peace, strength, and hope as you move forward. And may you always carry with you the beautiful memories and the love that will forever remain in your heart. With God, we will make it through grief.

In times of grief, the Word of God can be a source of profound comfort and strength. Scriptures remind us of God's promises, His presence, and His unwavering love, even in our darkest moments. Meditating on these scriptures-reading them, praying over them, and reflecting on their truth-can help soothe the heart, bring peace to the mind, and renew your spirit. Grief is a journey, and as you face the waves of emotions, leaning on the Word of God can anchor your soul.

Here are some powerful scriptures to encourage and uplift you in this season of loss. Take time to meditate on them, allowing their truth to speak to your heart again and again.

Psalm 73:26 ESV *"My flesh and my heart may fail, but God is the strength of my heart and my portion forever."*

John 16:22 NIV *"So with you: Now is your time of grief, but I will see you again and you will rejoice, and no one will take away your joy."*

Philippians 4:13 KJV *"I can do all things through Christ which strengtheneth me."*

Revelation 21:4 KJV *"And God shall wipe away all tears from their eyes; and there shall be no more death, neither sorrow, nor crying, neither shall there be any more pain: for the former things are passed away."*

Romans 8:18 NLT *"Yet what we suffer now is nothing compared to the glory he will reveal to us later."*

Psalm 34:18 ESV *"The Lord is near to the brokenhearted and saves the crushed in spirit."*

Psalm 73:26 KJV *"My flesh and my heart faileth: but God is the strength of my heart, and my portion forever."*

Matthew 5:4 KJV *"Blessed are they that mourn: for they shall be comforted."*

Matthew 11:28-30 NIV *"Come to me, all you who are weary and burdened, and I will give you rest. Take my yoke upon you and learn from me, for I am gentle and humble in heart, and you will find rest for your souls. For my yoke is easy and my burden is light."*

Isaiah 53:4-6 NIV *"Surely he took up our pain and bore our suffering, yet we considered him punished by God, stricken by him, and afflicted. But he was pierced for our transgressions, he was crushed for our iniquities; the punishment that brought us peace was on him, and by his wounds we are healed. We all, like sheep, have gone astray, each of us has turned to our own way; and the Lord has laid on him the iniquity of us all."*

Joshua 1:9 KJV *"Have not I commanded thee? Be strong and of a good courage; be not afraid, neither be thou dismayed: for the Lord thy God is with thee whithersoever thou goest."*

Isaiah 41:10 ESV *"Fear not, for I am with you; be not dismayed, for I am your God; I will strengthen you, I will help you, I will uphold you with my righteous right hand."*

John 14:27 NIV *"Peace I leave with you; my peace I give you. I do not give to you as the world gives. Do not let your hearts be troubled and do not be afraid."*

James 1:2-3 NIV *"Consider it pure joy, my brothers and sisters, whenever you face trials of many kinds, because you know that the testing of your faith produces perseverance."*

Proverbs 3:5-6 KJV *"Trust in the Lord with all thine heart; and lean not unto thine own understanding. In all thy ways acknowledge him, and he shall direct thy paths."*

2 Corinthians 1:3-4 NIV *"Praise be to the God and Father of our Lord Jesus Christ, the Father of compassion and the God of all comfort, who comforts us in all our troubles, so that we can comfort those in any trouble with the comfort we ourselves receive from God."*

Unbroken Key Takeaways

- The legacy left behind by loved ones, such as Dante's, can continue to impact others positively.

- Grief can coexist with celebration. In the midst of sorrow, honoring the life of a loved one—through actions like giving back to the community or sharing memories—can bring healing and joy.

- The first year after a loved one's passing is particularly challenging. Each holiday and milestone becomes a reminder of their absence, but it's an opportunity to create new ways to keep their memory alive.

- Don't wait to express love or appreciation for those you care about. Share your feelings, offer gratitude, and celebrate them while they can still experience your love.

- Honoring someone's life is about carrying forward their values and dreams.

Unbroken Reflection Questions:

1. How can you honor the loved ones in your life—both while they are here and after they've passed? What are meaningful ways to celebrate their legacy?

2. What personal values or dreams do you want to carry forward to leave a positive impact on others?

3. How can you transform grief into something positive, like giving back or creating meaningful traditions that honor those you've lost?

4. In what ways do you express love and appreciation for the people who matter to you? Are there any gestures you could do today to show them how much they mean to you?

5. What are some ways you can ensure the legacy of those who have passed continues to have a lasting effect in your community or your life?

RESOURCES

GRIEF JOURNEY

Grief can feel isolating and overwhelming, but it's important to know that you don't have to face it alone. There are compassionate resources available to help you process your pain, find comfort, and take steps toward healing. Whether you're seeking professional guidance, connecting with others who understand your loss, or simply looking for tools to help you cope, support is available. Remember, grieving is a personal journey, and there's no right or wrong way to navigate it. Here are some valuable resources to provide support, guidance, and community as you walk through this difficult time:

Grief Counseling and Therapy

1. GriefShare

www.griefshare.org

A national grief support group offering a safe environment for people to talk about their grief and receive help from others who are going through similar experiences.

2. Therapists Specializing in Grief

www.psychologytoday.com; www.therapyden.com

Professional counselors who specialize in grief can provide individual therapy to help you process emotions and develop coping strategies. Look for a licensed therapist in your area who specializes in grief and loss. Websites like Psychology Today or TherapyDen allow you to filter by specialty.

3. The American Hospice Foundation

www.americanhospice.org

Offers grief support resources, including professional guidance and information on how to find grief support services in your area.

Books on Grief

1. *The Year of Magical Thinking"* by Joan Didion

A powerful memoir about the author's journey through grief after the sudden death of her husband.

2. *"It's OK That You're Not OK"* by Megan Devine

This book is a compassionate guide through grief, emphasizing that it's

normal not to be okay after a loss and offering ways to move through it.

3. *"Grief Observed"* by C.S. Lewis

A deeply personal account by C.S. Lewis following the death of his wife, exploring his pain, questions, and thoughts on loss.

Online Grief Support Groups

1. Grief in Common

www.griefincommon.com

This online support community allows people to share their grief journey, connect with others who have lost loved ones, and receive encouragement.

2. The Compassionate Friends

www.compassionatefriends.org

This organization offers support to families after the death of a child, through both in-person meetings and online support.

3. The Suicide Prevention Lifeline

www.suicidepreventionlifeline.org

This hotline offers support to those who have lost a loved one to suicide. They also provide grief counseling services.

Grief Apps and Online Tools

1. "My Grief Angels"

www.mygriefangels.com

An app designed to connect grieving individuals with a community of others who understand their experience.

2. "Grief: Support for Young Adults"

www.griefsupportyoungadults.com

An app focused on helping young adults (ages 18-30) cope with grief. It provides tips, resources, and coping tools.

Hotlines for Immediate Support

If you or someone you know is facing an immediate crisis, such as thoughts of self-harm, harm to others, or a life-threatening emergency, please do not hesitate to call 911 for urgent assistance. Emergency responders are trained to provide the necessary support and resources to ensure your safety during critical situations.

1. National Helpline for Grief Support

Call 1-800-273-8255 for immediate support if you are struggling with overwhelming grief, especially during moments of crisis.

2. Crisis Text Line

Text HOME to 741741 to connect with a trained crisis counselor for emotional support, including for grief-related distress.

Community Resources

1. Local Hospices and Grief Support Groups

Many hospice centers offer grief support groups that are open to the community, even for those who have not had a loved one pass under hospice care.

2. Churches and Faith-Based Support Groups

Many churches provide grief groups for those who are mourning. It's a safe space to express grief through prayer, scripture, and community support.

Journaling and Creative Expression

"The Grief Journal" by Litsa Williams and Stephanie R. Tullio

This guided journal provides prompts to help process your grief and express your emotions in a constructive way.

DOMESTIC VIOLENCE

Domestic violence can feel isolating and overwhelming, but it's important to remember that help is available, and you are not alone. No one deserves to live in fear or endure abuse, and there are resources and people who are ready to support you. Whether you're seeking safety, guidance, or a way to begin healing, there are organizations dedicated to providing the tools and support you need. Taking the first step to reach out for help can be difficult, but it can also be life changing. Here are some important resources for those affected by domestic violence. These organizations offer support, safety planning, and guidance for individuals seeking to escape abusive situations. This is just a starting point-don't hesitate to seek the help you need. You are worth it.

1. National Domestic Violence Hotline (USA)

www.thehotline.org

Phone: 1-800-799-SAFE (7233)

The National Domestic Violence Hotline offers confidential support to individuals who are experiencing domestic violence, providing resources, safety planning, and connection to local shelters.

2. Domestic Violence Shelter and Advocacy Programs

Safe Horizon (New York)

www.safehorizon.org

A leading provider of support services to victims of domestic violence, including emergency shelters, legal advocacy, and counseling.

3. National Coalition Against Domestic Violence (NCADV)

www.ncadv.org

This organization provides resources for survivors, including information on safety planning, escaping abuse, and finding local support groups.

4. Women's Shelters

www.domesticshelters.org

Many local domestic violence shelters provide emergency housing, resources, and advocacy for survivors of domestic violence. This site helps over two million survivors each year.

5. Legal Assistance and Advocacy

www.legalaid.org

This website provides options for legal aid for victims of domestic violence. Many local and state legal aid organizations offer free legal assistance for survivors of domestic violence, including help with obtaining protective orders, custody issues, and other legal matters related to abuse.

6. National Immigration Legal Services (for immigrant victims)

www.immigrantjustice.org

This resource helps immigrant survivors of domestic violence navigate legal issues related to immigration and abuse.

7. Support for Children Affected by Domestic Violence

www.childwelfare.gov

Child Welfare Information Gateway

A service provided by the U.S. Department of Health & Human Services, offering resources for parents and caregivers of children who have been affected by domestic violence.

8. National Children's Alliance

www.nationalchildrensalliance.org

Provides resources and support for children who have been exposed to domestic violence, including information about child advocacy centers.

9. Hotlines for Immediate Assistance

National Domestic Violence Hotline

Call or text the National Domestic Violence Hotline for confidential support and safety planning.

Phone: 1-800-799-SAFE (7233)

Text: "START" to 88788

10. National Suicide Prevention Lifeline (if you are in immediate crisis and need emotional support)

Phone: 1-800-273-TALK (8255)

11. Loveisrespect (for teens and young adults)

www.loveisrespect.org

Loveisrespect provides 24/7 support for those in abusive relationships, especially for young people navigating dating violence.

Phone: 1-866-331-9474

Text: Text "LOVEIS" to 22522

12. Counseling and Therapy

www.psychologytoday.com

Therapists Specializing in Domestic Violence

Therapy can be a crucial part of healing after experiencing domestic violence. Search for therapists who specialize in trauma or abuse recovery through websites such as Psychology Today or TherapyDen.

13. The National Center on Domestic Violence, Trauma, & Mental Health

www.nationalcenterdvtraumamh.org

This site provides resources for mental health professionals and survivors, including strategies for addressing trauma and mental health impacts.

14. Online Support Groups and Communities

Pandora's Project (Online Support Group)

www.pandys.org

An online community for survivors of domestic violence, offering peer support, advice, and resources to help individuals heal.

15. Reddit's Domestic Violence Support Community

www.reddit.com/r/domesticviolence

A safe, anonymous space where survivors can discuss their experiences and support one another.

16. Emergency Safety Plans and Resources

www.thehotline.org/help/path-to-safety

National Domestic Violence Hotline's Safety Plan Guide

This tool helps you create a personalized safety plan for leaving an abusive relationship.

17. Safety Planning for Domestic Violence

www.domesticshelters.org/safety-planning

Many shelters and advocacy groups provide personalized safety planning for individuals in unsafe relationships.

18. For Men Affected by Domestic Violence

www.1in6.org](https://www.1in6.org)

This organization offers resources, support, and counseling specifically for men who are survivors of domestic violence or sexual abuse.

JOURNALING

Journaling can be a powerful tool for coping with grief and finding a path toward healing. It provides a safe space to express the emotions that may feel overwhelming to share out loud, offering clarity and release in moments of confusion, sadness, or anger. Writing allows you to process your thoughts, honor your feelings, and reflect on the memories and lessons connected to your loved one. Through journaling, you can uncover moments of gratitude, find strength in the midst of pain, and begin to piece together a new reality while still cherishing the life and love you've lost. Here are some grief journal prompts to help individuals process their emotions, reflect on their journey, and find healing during a difficult time:

1. Feelings and Emotions

- How do I feel today?

- What emotions are most present?

- What are some things that I've tried to avoid thinking about?

- Why am I avoiding them?

- Are there any feelings or emotions that surprise me during this grieving process?

- What do I think they're telling me?

- What are the things I wish I could say to my loved one if they were here right now?

2. Remembering the Loved One

- What is my favorite memory of the person I lost?

- If I could spend one more day with my loved one, what would we do together?

- What would I say to them?

- What is something about them that made me smile?

- Write about the little things that made them unique.

- How would they want me to feel right now?

3. Healing and Coping

- What has helped me feel a little better during my grief journey?

- Is there something I could do more that brings comfort?

- How do I take care of myself when I'm feeling overwhelmed by grief?

- Are there things that I need to start doing to take better care of myself?

- What does self-compassion look like to me right now?

- How can I show myself more kindness during this difficult time?

- What have I learned about myself through the grieving process?

4. Guilt and Regret

- Are there any unresolved feelings or things I wish I would have said or done?

- How can I forgive myself for those things?

- Have I felt guilty for continuing to live life or find happiness? Why or why not?

- If I could ask my loved one for forgiveness, or to make peace, what would I want to say?

5. Navigating Special Occasions

- How do I feel about celebrating holidays, birthdays, and/or anniversaries without my loved one?

- How can I honor my loved one on important dates or milestones in a way that feels right for me?

- What is one new tradition I could start to remember and celebrate my loved one's life?

6. Impact on Relationships

- How has my grief affected my relationships with family and friends?

- Is there anything I need to express to them or ask for?

- Who has been there for me during my grief, and how have they shown up for me?

- Are there relationships I feel more distant from since my loss? Why do I think that is?

- How can I approach healing in these relationships?

7. Spirituality and Faith

- How has my faith or spiritual beliefs been impacted by my grief?

- What have I struggled with in my faith journey?

- Have I experienced any moments of connection or peace that I believe were signs from my loved one or from God?

- What are my requests from God, or my spiritual practices, to continue healing?

- How can I lean on my faith to find hope again in the midst of my pain?

8. Acceptance and Moving Forward

- What does "moving forward" look like to me?
- Does it mean letting go, or is it something different?
- What would it look like to continue honoring my loved one while also living my own life?
- How do I know when I'm ready to take steps forward in my healing process?
- What are my fears about moving forward, and how can I begin to face them?

9. Personal Growth Through Grief

- How has this loss changed me?
- What parts of myself have I discovered or rediscovered?
- What strength have I found in myself that I didn't know I had before?
- How can I use my experience with grief to support others who are grieving or going through something difficult?
- What are some positive things I've learned about love, life, and loss through this process?

10. Messages and Letters

- Write a letter to your loved one, expressing your current thoughts and feelings.
- Write a letter to yourself, reminding yourself of your strength, the healing journey, and that it's okay to have bad days.

- If you could give your grief a name, what would it be and why?

11. Dreams and Hopes for the Future

- What do I want my life to look like as I move forward in my grief journey?

- What are my dreams for the future?

- How can I build a future where both my grief and my joy coexist?

- What would a healthy, healed version of myself look like, and how can I take steps toward becoming that person?

WORKS CITED

American Psychological Association. "Domestic Violence and
Marginalized Groups." *American Psychological Association*,
https://www.apa.org/pi/women/resources/violence

Centers for Disease Control and Prevention. *National Intimate
Partner and Sexual Violence Survey.* CDC,
https://www.cdc.gov/violenceprevention/datasources/nisvs/index.h
tml

Journal of Family Violence. "Discrimination and Domestic
Violence." *SpringerLink*

https://link.springer.com/journal/10896

National Domestic Violence Hotline. "Domestic Violence
Statistics." *The Hotline*

https://www.thehotline.org/

Substance Abuse and Mental Health Services Administration.
"Behavioral Health Equity for Black Men." *SAMHSA*
https://www.samhsa.gov/

Violence Policy Center. "Black Homicide Victimization." *Violence
Policy Center*

https://vpc.org/

Connect with the Author

Instagram: @marciancole

Facebook: @marciancole

Youtube: @marciancole

Email: hello@marciancole.com

Join her growing faith community, where she leads a weekly Bible study, hosts daily morning calls for intentional time with God, and facilitates engaging Thursday night Zoom talks.

www.bit.ly/marciaspeaks

Instagram: @faithfocusfinishstrong

www.ingramcontent.com/pod-product-compliance
Lightning Source LLC
Chambersburg PA
CBHW050448150626
46551CB00029B/1986